ITALIAN POLITICS EXPLAINED TO MY DAUGHTER

How to gain seats of power in Italy

FRANZ PAGOT

The Perfect Edition c/o PPI WORLDWIDE ltd
Office 311 Winston House - 2 Dollis Park Finchley
London N3 1HF United Kingdom

www.theperfectedition.com

To Luisa,
who has never wanted the spotlight,
but who has made so many others shine.

From the same author:
FAILED ANGELS
WARZONE GHOSTS
IMMERSIVE 3-D
ERMM...
GREENHORN

In print:
WET THE BABY'S HEAD
SIDEEFFX
BEDDA MATRI (THE BEAUTIFUL MOTHER)

CONTENTS

ACKNOWLEDGEMENTS

A long time ago, somebody wrote that it's a good idea to avoid writing acknowledgements at the beginning of a book because they violate the intimate relationship between the writer and the reader.

So, here are my acknowledgements. I'm sure that you want to keep your distance, and don't worry, I'm not offended.

My children, Elena and Enrico, are the real inspiration for this book. It was them who encouraged me to collect our conversations in a single volume that can be read by young people, fostering in them a love for politics and a commitment not to reject it *a priori*.

I thank my wife Cristina who provided a welcome touch of comic relief to brighten up the hard times, but who has, in fact, always been my strict and meticulous (but never fastidious!) editor, even in life.

Thanks to Cinzia De Martin: your doubts encouraged me to clarify some passages, so you can rest easy now.

"Grazie" to Lauren O'Hagan who translated the English version. Aristotle would be surely proud of it.

I'm also grateful to Elena's classmates who added interesting questions, particularly Eleonora Furlan, Gemma Tolin and Maja Dall'Acqua; I can't thank Pietro, Michele and Chiara because they never existed.

A heartfelt thanks to Veronica Daniele, Elena's long-time childhood friend, who provided her valuable opinion and earnt herself a steak to balance her salad-based diet. Come to lunch whenever you want.

Thanks also to her father Duilio, a brilliant humourist (unbeknown to him!), reluctant writer and dear tatami friend.

I owe an enormous debt to Dario Pettinelli, a journalist with a sharp pen and a great nose.

I'm infinitely grateful to Maurizio Costanzo. A book with his foreword instantly becomes a classic. I hope to live up to it.

But my deepest and most heartfelt thanks go to my sister Luisa, who tried to kill me with an iron when we were kids, but spared me, foreseeing that one day we'd do great things together.

The beauty of political scientists is that, by the time they answer, nobody can remember what they were asked.

(Indro Montanelli)

FOREWORD

by Maurizio Costanzo

Talking about politics has never been easy because it's a bit like getting naked: you reveal an important part of your thoughts, of your life choices.

In times like these, when the world of politics has sadly accustomed us to frequent and sudden transformations, it's hard to understand what's really left or right, or even what politics is in general.

Added to the reticence of our ideologies, which makes us talk cautiously about our political orientation, there's the confusion of class politics, where people come together today only to fall apart tomorrow.

When you hear a politician speak – whether they're right or left wing, radical or moderate – you feel eager to embrace their ideas, support their proposals because, after all, everybody uses their election manifestos to claim that they're acting for the good of the country, for the community.

5

When you're good at telling stories, it seems like everybody is a nice guy.

Of course, people have the freedom to change their opinions, but if you think about it, having many shared ideologies or having many different ideologies is a bit like having none at all, especially when nobody can resist the ones that are extolled.

We often discuss politics or hear politics being discussed as if we've been left behind by fifty years or more.

When clinging to old political settings that no longer have reason to exist today, we should ask ourselves whether it's not the very idea of politics that has changed and the very concept of party which has strayed far from its original meaning.

Parties once derived from so-called class struggles.

Social hardships exploded into reactionary movements and parties were nothing more than an organised and non-violent way of expressing these hardships.

I don't feel nostalgic about old politics or old parties; on the contrary, I'd like individuals to move with the times and not persist in proposing old tactics that no longer represent anybody.

Above all, politics must address young people, but this can't be done properly if we fail to realise that the children of this Republic have changed a lot.

The finger is often pointed at the younger generations. They're accused of being poorly informed and not at all interested in politics.

But I believe that it's the other way round: politics has little interest in young people.

If I were 18 today and watched a political programme to get more information and make sure that I exercised my right to vote in the best possible way, I'd probably find myself feeling even more confused because, too often, I get the feeling that I hear good things, but these things are actually the lesser of two evils.

Young people deserve attention and consideration.

The relationship between politics and young people should be a bit like what Franz Pagot captures in this book, between a father and a daughter.

A teenage daughter who asks her father one of the most common questions: "Who do you vote for?"

Every politician, but I also mean every adult, should imagine being that father who willingly tries to make young people understand that politics – real politics – is a noble tool through which things can be changed to improve their future, their life.

INTRODUCTION

Without doubt, I blame Aristotle.

The great thinker, born in Stagira, has unquestionably influenced the way that politics is done in the West more than Socrates, who was unbeatable in debate and a valiant soldier on the battlefield, but who left nothing in writing. The sayings we attribute to Socrates actually come from Plato, who added his own twist, and we all know that attention-seeking is the wildest and most devious way to censor somebody else's work.

Socrates is still my hero, but Aristotle has left a purer and clearer impression; he also served as tutor to that genius Alexander the Great, thereby playing a key role in his formative education. And it was Aristotle who stated that man is by nature a political animal, and Aristotle himself who reassured everybody by saying: *If there is a solution, why are you worried? If there is no solution, why are you worried?*

My daughter looked at me like Giulio Andreotti looked at that glass of water that Bettino Craxi passed him in a debate.

It was the gaze of somebody who has no choice but to trust, even if they're doubtful.

"Dad, I only asked you why I understand practically nothing when it comes to politics in Italy. What does the nemesis of us high school students have to do with it?"

You'll find the rest of this conversation later on, but I wanted to blame somebody immediately. That's the favourite sport of all us Italians, not just of many politicians.

The blame for this book, which is not particularly honest (and I'll explain why later on), is entirely mine. After thirty years of living abroad – particularly in London – working in cinema and advertising, I suddenly feel a duty to give my daughter a clearer idea of how politics works in Italy. To sum up by using somebody else's words (typical of politics!): *politics in Italy is serious, but can't be taken seriously.* And this was stated by good old Ennio Flaiano – a popular screenwriter and novelist – back in the 1960s. Since then, stupidity has come on leaps and bounds.

As an emigrant, I agree with Flaiano who said that Italy is a country that is like a campsite for Italians. As elections come around, this becomes even more apparent, since everybody wants to follow the herd, regardless of the colours they wear.

This dusty whirlwind of change and U-turns in a country where black turns red faster than in a game of roulette transforms any attempt at explanation – understood as the act of making clear what is unclear – into a foolish but also brave act.

But we're brave not when we have all the answers, but when we face the questions we've always tried to avoid. Then we can no longer deceive ourselves. So, here's my first lie: I am not going to explain anything. We are going to simply discuss together, dear readers, talk to each other. Just as I did with my daughter. Let's talk about Elena then, since I haven't introduced her yet. She was born in London – just like her brother was four years earlier – and she now studies in Italy. She's in the penultimate year of *Liceo Classico* – a type of high school focused on humanities – and getting excellent grades. At home, we mainly talk the language of Queen Elizabeth and we read everything in both Italian and English. We watch CNN and the BBC, and read other newspapers, whether Italian or foreign, including *Le Monde*. I wouldn't want to treat the French wrongly seeing as, when it comes to revolutions, they understand them more than anyone else. I often discuss foreign politics with Enrico, who is a medical student in Milan.

We particularly talk about American politics as it so rich in material and so funny since Donald Trump became president. My son has a dry sense of humour like a true Brit and the conversations we have are often fun, even when they conceal serious concerns. Don't think, however, that we have big discussions.

On the whole, we don't talk about politics, especially at the dining table. Just like scientists who dine together: knowledgeable away from the table but respectful at the dining table.

Pasta and *Brunello* wine provide the best answers for both palates and the most demanding brains.

The question that all parents fear from their children, almost more than *can you lend me the car?* is *how should I vote?*

Any mishaps caused by this answer, when wrong, will have repercussions for years to come. And as with all difficult questions, a question that has no answer is preferable to a question that requires one. Unfortunately, copying the skills of a word warrior like dear Socrates is useless with a teenager who goes to a *Liceo Classico*. You manage to deliver a fake jab, but then she knocks you out with a *one-two* that leaves you gasping like a fish out of water. Let's stick with that image of the sea. I've always equated explaining Italian politics to an attempt to do synchronised swimming in a Force 7 sea: not only impossible, but rather dangerous. Yet here I am, a reckless sailor taking the ship's helm against the wind, directing logic where few fearless people dare, especially if like me, they have no qualifications to do so, not even braiding on their jacket.

"Are you a *Homo Novus*?" asked my daughter.

"What do you mean?" I said, hiding a certain nervousness, since it sounded so novice.

"I mean that you're involved in politics even though you come from a humble non-political background," she said with a smile.

True, this poor *homo sapiens* comes from a modest family.

My father was a typographer and my mother was a house-wife, but I was surrounded by piles of books that my father took home from the printers to proofread. To this day, if books don't cover my walls, I feel the draughts of ignorance giving me shivers, and you can die of ignorance, ladies and gentlemen. When I was a child, we never really discussed politics in my house. My father Bruno had liberal views and was the most honest person I've ever known, to the point that he gave me a huge slap when I triumphantly brought home a 50,000 lire banknote that I found in the churchyard. I had to go back to the crime scene and hand it over to the parish priest because *somebody*, my father yelled, was sure to be desperately looking for it to feed their children. The priest promised to keep it safe, away from thieves like me, prescribing a couple of Hail Marys to mark the occasion that would heal the stain on my teenage soul.

Writers with firm and rigid ideas about Mussolini came to visit us at home, but so too did intellectuals in red scarves.

Regardless of their colours, all agreed that my mother was an excellent cook who, as a good Neapolitan, could silence every-body with her ladle. My father was highly respected at work and in the local community and received pressure from all sides to enter politics, but we hardly ever talked about it. It was an unwritten law that we never discussed work, politics or religion, especially at the dining table. Never. Ever.

And since my father was a hyperactive workaholic, lunch and

13

dinner were the only times we could talk. This peace lasted for a long time until a dear family friend – a diehard communist, amateur boxer and professional trade unionist – came to lunch and forgot what not to do at the table. Thanks to Finagle's Law – an appendix to Murphy's Law that states *anything that can go wrong will at the worst possible moment* – he shouted words that were more offensive than a belch: "So Bruno, why don't you join the Communist Party? Christ on a bike, we really need people like you!"

The minestrone suddenly turned stone cold.

Spoons and jaws hovered in mid-air.

The blasphemy in that sentence was in good company.

My father didn't get upset. He just put his spoon on his plate and stated, "I'd also like to be a communist. It's just that I can't afford it!" His spoon remained on his plate, while our tongues descended to the ground, shocked by such unusual calm.

Years passed where political struggle was both fierce and incomprehensible, especially when I was beaten up once for being dressed in black and once for wearing a red shirt that an aunt gave me. To this day, I think that she knew exactly what she was doing. In any case, I confess that politics has always fascinated me.

I've always tried to understand the different points of view that are often confused by deliberately obscure and convoluted language, which is amusing because it's often peppered with blunders by those who confuse Aristotelian pathos (the genius of Stagira is back!) with the goose we call pâté.

Little gems like *I'll be short, even circumcised*, accidentally stated instead of 'concise'. Or the time when a well-known paediatrician was pompously introduced to the citizens gathered in the square as *The greatest paedophile in Italy!* I'll stop right here so as not to rub salt in the *wombs*.

I'll refrain from recalling the politicians who slipped ruinously on Cicero's tongue, creating incoherent mumbo jumbo that *Liceo Classico* pupils in particular find to be irresistible comedy. The English spoken by our government representatives is something else and there's no way to rinse it in the Thames to make it more presentable, with all due respect to Alessandro Manzoni who worried about "rinsing his clothes in the Arno" – an expression he coined to describe his trip to Florence to immerse himself in Florentine dialect and, therefore, purify *The Betrothed* with a more refined Italian.

Anyway, I was talking about my daughter.

Young people today don't like politics or, even worse, are horrified by it. Countless recent studies have analysed the dynamics of politics.

Emeritus psychologists and sociologists have unveiled theories and theses that flood the internet, not just bookstores. Yet nobody admits that the reasons are simple and spontaneous, just like a baby burping after being fed.

Young people today say that politicians do nothing.

They always fight over the same things. Nobody is sincere. And especially those who govern us are not interested in solving problems; they only want to hold firmly onto power.

To be fair, this is not always the case, but perception is reality in today's world where image counts more than substance. Just add a label and you're branded.

On the topic of politicians' dishonesty (or lack thereof), to be fair, I'd distinguish between those who are truly honest, those who are honest when the stakes are small and those who are always dishonest. They say that opportunity makes a man a thief, but often, it's necessity that makes a man a thief, or the crooks he keeps company with, who, in turn, create the opportunity to be thieves. In what capacity then do I dare to explain the tangled and indistinct skein of Italian politics? A skein that is more like a foul-smelling, badly digested bolus than *bucatini* pasta with cheese and peppers.

I blame the English.

And just to err on the side of caution, I blame the Americans too. In fact, it's my years as an emigrant with a proudly Italian passport that has turned me into a protector that defends all things Italian from those foreigners who are so loved by us Italians. We've always been Anglophiles and Hollywood buffs, long before spaghetti westerns even made their way onto this media and culture scene that favours *Yankees and gentlemen.*

I've been a forced spokesperson for Italy, where pizzas and mandolins are no longer enough to silence curiosity about the acrobatics of Italian politics.

My life on the film set of English-language productions is made up of much travelling and staying in hotels. A circus life where spaces and thoughts are shared: reflections on cultures and customs, opinions on political and non-political figures. The question that I've had to answer most often is "Did you vote for Berlusconi?" along with "Why did Berlusconi get into politics?"

My daughter asked me the same question and you'll have to trawl through a lot of pages before you find the answer, swimming between oxymorons and metonymies, metaphors and euphemisms. In any case, I'll spare you the swathes of useless hyperbole – a technique so beloved in the world of politics. I'm not going to sort these conversation notes into any particular order. I'm not going to arrange them by topic.

I'm going to respect what we love most in kids and what we lose so quickly once we become adults: spontaneity.

This is not a written tool for young people who want to get into politics; rather, it's bait to bring young people closer to politics, show them its fascinating contradictions, balances and, above all, dynamics in the hope that they participate more and change things for the better, become more involved.

This little book's dishonesty is not intentional, but innate when the word *explain* is added to *politics* in the title.

This is an oxymoron, given that the two words contradict one another, not only in terms of their opposing meanings but also their vested right of abuse and misappropriation.

Fortunately, my daughter is here to brighten everything up. Her spontaneity and uncorrupted honesty, her mind which is accustomed to two languages at the same time, not to mention that concept that the Japanese like so much: *shoshin*, that is, emptying the mind of knowledge acquired in the past and being willing to replace old knowledge with new information. And I expect this from you, dear readers.

Whether you are political veterans, internationally renowned scholars, shrewd journalists or unscrupulous lobbyists, I ask you for once to walk the corridors of power with me to suss out and understand its mechanisms through the eyes of a curious teenager. And if you're still wondering how I, a man of cinema, have learnt the secrets of Parliament or have worked out its mysteries, don't fear.

The answer is very simple and you'll find it at the end of this book.

But be honest and don't cheat, at least this time: young people are watching you.

1. REVOLUTION

My daughter was watching me with amused eyes.

She certainly wasn't expecting such a shocked reaction from me. After all, she had only asked a simple question, just like thousands of other times before on our cobblestone walks together. Cobblestones which, when dislodged and loose, remind me so much of mass revolutions when people use them as deadly projectiles. The most dangerous question she had asked me so far had been *does Santa Claus exist?* which she whispered with a face full of fear many years ago.

Right from the very start, my wife and I decided to always be open and accessible to our children, never lying to them, or at least as little as possible. And I must admit that at the time I thought I'd done well. I replied that good old Santa Claus exists as long as we want him to exist. Sometimes we just need to believe in something because the very thought that a myth might be true brings comfort and joy.

Proving its existence or not is irrelevant.

I also added that the *magic* of Christmas comes from the fact that many children strongly believe in Santa Claus.

But this time it was different. I wouldn't get let off the hook so easily. The question was much deeper.

"Who are you voting for?"

Ouch! The weight of my possible answer came down on me like a ton of bricks, each one of them unleashing both individual and collective pain. My first reaction was to reply that voting is secret and personal, but I quickly realised that in a family like ours, where we've always insisted that there are no secrets and that everybody is free to debate, declaring that something was private would have been pure hypocrisy. I also suddenly realised that I no longer remembered – totally and utterly no longer remembered – what and for whom I had voted. How is that possible? You might ask.

I clearly remember receiving the ballot paper in the post, as is the case for us emigrants, and spreading it out on the table. It was full of all sorts of ugly symbols and kinds of feasible names, even if the names printed on the pastel-coloured sheet seemed more suited to an old label on a bottle of a cough medicine than to the modern political scene.

I'll also confess that I thought some of them had already moved on to a better place, and I'm not talking about the Senate!

"I don't remember..." was the sincerest answer I could give and the one that actually made its way out of my mouth.

My daughter's astonishment was equally sincere. "How can you not remember such a thing, *babbo*?!"

I felt like a defendant standing before the prosecution in a detective film. My daughter's eyes were scrutinising every possible sign that betrayed the truthfulness of my version of an unlikely event.

"I don't remember!" I reiterated with the conviction of somebody admitting to themselves that their memory has played a bad trick – a very skillful and cruel trick – on the typical timing of sadistic humour at the worst possible moment.

"You see," I added, "Lately, it's been hard to follow people who represent ideals that were carried like a banner up until a few years ago. Ideals that were fiercely defended with *never evers* and then the never evers suddenly surrendered like sandcastles in the first parliamentary *squall.*"

"What do you mean by parliamentary squall? And how does Parliament work? How does politics work in Italy?"

There are moments, I thought, when you realise that eternity is a really long time, especially towards the end.

Explain Italian politics? Are you having a laugh?

You know that moment when the police stop you for speeding and your brain starts working even faster to come up with a credible excuse, but your brain's cogs slip on the wet surface of your nervous sweat? Well, I felt that way now.

But my brain was also descending into a whirlpool of contradictory thoughts coming from the opposite side.

I decided to take it slowly: what do you know about how the government works? Don't they teach you the Constitution at school? Calling *liceo* "school" when talking to a liceo pupil is like calling a great and famous professor of medicine "doctor": he would look at you with the contempt and superiority of somebody with a deep knowledge of things to which only a few humans have privileged access. My question was met with a teenage snort. I had only asked it to buy me some time. In the breeze, I followed the flash of her intense green eyes, which had just studied Xenophon in his original language, Ancient Greek, which looks like Cyrillic to most people. In this first round, the cards weren't stacked in my favour. In the past, when I got in the ring, I never even thought about losing, but sparring with a seventeen-year-old daughter means that I'll lose the exchange of blows even before the end of round bell has rung. As usual, I decided to treat her like the woman she is, not the little girl who every father wants to jealously protect from a corrupt and confused world. However, I also sighed. It was the sigh of a fifty-year-old on the ropes.

Then I set the record straight.

"Okay, so let's assume that you have the basics, or at least promise me that you'll Google them. I can tell you what the books don't say, what many people don't know and, above all, what I discovered thanks to my informants."

I added this last phrase to make myself sound a bit important. I had always liked hearing it said by the heroes in *Starsky & Hutch*. Who doesn't love the best informant of all TV informants: Huggy Bear? But back to us in the ring.

"Informants?" It was her fake jab.

"You mean my aunt?"

I warned you that her one-two was dangerous.

I took the blow and attacked from the side.

"Let's concentrate," I said, "And I'll explain how politics works, but don't expect me to explain *who* is involved in politics too. I can't do that."

"There's not much to explain. My classmates say that they all suck and one of my classmates says that his dad wants Mussolini back, and he agrees." I took a deep breath.

"Forget whoever wants the return of coloured shirts and scarves," I answered slowly. "Whatever colour they are, they end up being used to hang people, even upside down."

"Why don't you want to explain politicians to me? Surely, it's better to get to know the politicians first and, as a result, understand politics?"

I replied with a smile. "If you understand the political mechanism, you understand *who* is involved in politics. It may not be any simpler, but it might be more accessible, provided that you ignore certain prejudices and accept that, as André Malraux said, *You don't enter politics with morals, or without them, for that matter.*"

"That doesn't make sense, Dad. It's like saying you don't build a house with bricks, but you don't build it without them either."

"That's right. In fact, it takes an architect, builders, wood, glass and steel, not to mention mortar and concrete; bricks are not a house."

Rolling her eyes, my daughter fixed her hair, typical of somebody preparing an attack. "Dad, that's just being creative with language!"

"I don't deny that, but it makes us think that we can't understand politics without accepting that politics is part of man, just as bricks are part of a house. Saying *I don't do politics* is like saying *I don't live.*"

"Aristotle again, *babbo*?"

"No, although he could have easily said that. The person who said it was Jules Renard."

"Malraux... Renard... what's with all these French people? We're not talking about revolution!"

"Renard was a fine connoisseur of the human soul, a witty and subtle philosopher with some beautiful sayings, the most famous being: *laziness is nothing more than the habit of resting before you get tired.*"

Elena didn't miss a trick. "That suits politicians perfectly."

"Relying too much on clichés and prejudices is the first mistake that people who want to understand make. And speaking of understanding, not only was Malraux a great writer – he wrote *Man's Fate* – but he was also twice a minister. He travelled all over the world and did great things both as a writer – one of his books was adapted into a film – and as a politician."

"I'd prefer it if there were revolutionaries. Many of my classmates say that it would take a good revolution to sort out Italy."

I burst out laughing.

"Italy is not a country of revolutionaries. Its people do not take to the streets! The typical Italian is too easily satisfied. Just give him a game of football on TV on Sundays and brioche every morning and he's fine: *bread and circuses*, as Juvenal said."

"To be fair, *babbo*, Italy has had its revolutions. *The Risorgimento* – the Italian unification – for example…"

I interrupted her. "No, don't give me the school version. The *Risorgimento* was not some heroic moment with a handful of unblemished heroes. They had plenty of blemishes.

And it was also full of larger-than-life characters who craved attention and sought retaliation, causing unnecessary damage and deaths. We are a country of emigrants thanks to the *Risorgimento*, which plundered wealth left, right and centre, regardless of the consequences. In any case, even if we considered the Risorgimento to be a real revolution, we never finished it. Instead, we left it halfway like almost all people's initiatives, including democracy and the Constitution. We Italians can only finish works of art, even if we then let them fall into ruin. When the *Carbonari* – the secret revolutionary societies – tried to involve the working classes, it all ended very badly, since the people didn't actually support them. A united Italy didn't come from the revolution of Italians barricaded in the street; it came from the genius of Cavour, who followed the directives of Victor Emmanuel II's monarchy. Italians only make barricades if they can use other people's furniture. They might put out a cooking pot, at most."

My daughter looked at me as if she were a supporter of Garibaldi who had just been served rationed slop. I increased the dose.

"As the writer Leo Longanesi said: *we Italians would like to have a revolution with the permission of the Carabinieri!*"

"I can't believe that you would reduce the *Risorgimento* to this. If only my teacher heard you! Anyway, everybody is always quoting history, as if nothing can be discussed without bringing up the past."

I was waiting for my daughter to say this. I was waiting for her right at the crossing as if we were standing at Porta Pia during the Capture of Rome.

"History is the only thing that can teach us something. It's the teacher of life so that we don't repeat the mistakes of the past. If you look at history, you realise that the most dangerous thing in politics is to flaunt nostalgia as if it were something new. We look at the past as if it were immersed in a gold dust that smells of roses when, in fact, it often smells like a cesspit of lies drunk greedily by the masses. You often hear the saying that history repeats itself, but this is actually not the case at all. Yes, there are themes that recur, but history is too complex to repeat itself."

My daughter kept looking at me in disbelief.

"So, let's do this," I continued, "Let's take an example of contemporary history: *Harry Potter*."

This time it was Elena who burst out laughing.

"Harry Potter is not history, *babbo*! It's fiction!"

"You see," I replied immediately, "You're only looking on the surface, you Harry Potter lover! Twelve publishing houses rejected J.K. Rowling's Harry Potter manuscript before the Bloomsbury president listened to his eight-year-old daughter Alice. Harry Potter was translated into 60 languages, distributed worldwide and earnt the author and publisher billions of dollars.

Can't you take a history lesson from that?"

With a smirk, she delivered her favourite blow: "The real lesson is that fathers should always listen to their daughters!"

"If Brutus had had a sister, Caesar would have died of old age!" I added, making her laugh again.

"But do you think women are better than men at politics?" she replied cunningly. Evidently, my pause was too long.

"Daddy? You don't agree?" she added with an air of annoyance.

"You know I don't like to say *better or worse*. It's always more complicated than that and it's limiting because we usually end up reducing everything to stereotypes by emphasising a gender characteristic. For example, women are more adept at getting people to agree on something, at finding a compromise, while men are more competitive and geared towards confrontation."

I noticed that she was getting irritated and decided to run for cover. "Do you know who Ginger Rogers was?"

"An actress?" she answered listlessly.

"Yes, but above all, she was an incredible tap dancer. Look for her videos and you'll see how amazing her movements were, especially when she danced with Fred Astaire, the best tap dancer ever. When she was asked what it felt like to dance with a star like Fred Astaire, she elegantly replied that on stage she did everything he did and, moreover, she did it backwards and in high heels."

Elena laughed heartily. "Then you agree with me!"

"You know that I'm a feminist!" I exclaimed, "There are many smart women in politics and in the government. Look at Angela Merkel, for example. But it makes no sense to say that women are better than men, even if I'd prefer there to be more women in high-level positions, not just in politics, but also in many other sectors, including filmmaking. Surely too much testosterone is counterproductive. I don't want to reduce everything to a male-female issue, but I hope that men start to appreciate more than just a beautiful pair of legs coming out of a skirt."

She laughed again.

"And in Italy, are there smart women in politics?"

She always managed to catch me off guard with her sudden questions. I saved myself as best I could.

"In Italy, Lina Merlin is remembered by everybody in my father's generation because she shut down the brothels, the closed houses of prostitutes. It's still a very contested law. She was an ex-partisan and anti-fascist who helped draft the Constitution. In fact, she added the sentence *without distinction of sex* to article three. She took away the difference between adopted children and actual children, as well as the *spinster clause* which meant that women who worked were fired when they got married."

"So, women could get fired just because they wanted to get married?"

"Yes. Remember that women in Italy were only granted the right to vote in general elections in 1946 and that it was Article 3 of the 1948 Italian Constitution that guaranteed equal rights and equal social status for women in every field. Another person who helped draft the Constitution was Nilde Iotti, who was highly respected and who became President of the Chamber of Deputies for several years. She's a symbol for emancipated women who are also successful in politics. Her role was then expertly taken up by Irene Pivetti more recently. A former primary school teacher called Tina Anselmi became the first female minister in our history. I think she was Minister of Labour, and then Minister of Health, and she fought tirelessly for the equal opportunities law. But the woman who is still considered to have had the biggest influence on Italian politics is Emma Bonino who fought some truly historic battles. Listing them all would take more than a whole afternoon. Just think that the American magazine *Newsweek* included her in their list of 150 women who shake the world."

"Wow, so she's also known abroad?"

"Of course. She was very active in Europe and was also a Member of the European Parliament in Brussels. Very accomplished internationally. She's always been known for her combative and nonconformist style.

She's a person with strong convictions who is always determined to go all the way, even if she makes enemies. I can't remember who, I think it was the former President of Italy, Sandro Pertini, who called her the *rascal of Montecitorio*."

"Was she really that *bad*?"

"In a good way, yes. She's still a real force of nature, passionate about freedom, democracy and justice, but even though she's much loved, she's never managed to translate that emotional consensus into votes."

"Because she's a woman?"

"I don't know. I honestly don't know. I'm convinced that there's no single answer. I mean, she was Minister of Foreign Affairs in 2013, and yet she finds it hard to get votes when she stands for election. For many, she's just an eternal candidate. When there was talk of her possibly becoming President of Italy, many expressed their support – in the world of politics but also in the world of entertainment – but ironically, nothing came of it. I think that many people associate her with issues like abortion, euthanasia and other secular matters that are frowned upon by Catholic Italy, which still rules the roost, despite a lot of talk about how it's high time for a female candidate."

"Depressing…" she said, showing me the Google search results on her mobile phone, after typing *best women in Italian politics*.

"Most of the results concern their appearance: *Miss Parliament: look and choose the most beautiful…* or: *Women in politics, the ten sexiest Italians…* Are we really only judged on the way we look?"

I shook my head. She was right. "Margaret Thatcher once said that true gender equality will come when a stupid woman takes the place of a stupid man without anyone noticing."

We laughed together. It was time for me to have a nice coffee and for my daughter to go back to studying Xenophon.

This chat with tinges of politics was the first of many, and it reached a point when even some of her schoolmates got involved. The tone of our conversations remained like the one you've just heard: a mixture of serious and well-ordered thoughts alternated with moments of chaos, which today's young people dare to call brainstorming, and which we at that age called making a mess. This was often said by teachers or parents, worried that our young minds would be corrupted by crazy and dangerous ideas, filling us with warnings and lists of things to do, which added to the already long dictates of things *not to do*.

Back then, they talked to us from high horses, without listening to what we had to say.

The real revolution in politics comes from young people. By listening to them.

2. LIMPING RUNNERS

William James, an American psychologist and philosopher of functionalism and pragmatism who was widely popular in Europe, wrote that a great many people think that they are thinking when they are merely rearranging their prejudices.

Thinking that all politicians are corrupt does nothing but feed this prejudice. It ignores facts and objective data to the detriment of those who make sacrifices for the good of others.

This attitude should be kept in mind when speaking to young people. It reminds us that the aggressive reluctance to discuss politics is the child of aversion to everything that is considered dirty or ugly, even if only perceived as such.

Young people's vision of the *homo politicus* today is very similar to that conjured up by the director Elio Petri in the 1970s, especially in films like *Investigation of a Citizen Above Suspicion*, or *Illustrious Corpses* by another great director from that period, Francesco Rosi.

"Why illustrious?" Elena put her arm around my neck, planting a kiss on my cheek.

"How did school go?" I asked.

"Illustrious, like a corpse!" she laughed as she sat down next to me, exaggerating her post-school fatigue.

"Was I talking to myself?" I asked, knowing full well the answer. Elena nodded even before I finished the sentence.

"*Illustrious* because it was important, above all. At that time, film production was exceptional in that respect. There was scathing criticism of the abuses of the powerful in the so-called *Anni di Piombo* – Years of Lead – the youth riots of the '70s and the exploitation for political purposes of a real social discontent. It was a very dark period in recent Italian history."

"Did they use young people's discontent for political purposes?"

"Of course, even if the vast majority of Italian politicians have always ignored or underestimated young people. Until a few years ago, we could count the exceptions on the fingers of one hand, and even the exceptions *used* young people to gain immediate approval, only to disregard their expectations later.

Sandro Pertini, the beloved President of Italy, had a straightforward and unconventional style. He was plain-speaking and always ready with a quip. He was an instinctive figure adored by the young people of the time. Many have now forgotten him, but he marked a new style of president, and he was even quite witty.

Young people liked him because, deep down, he was a pretend rough diamond, who played to what Italians do best: feel sympathy for those who appear simple and defenceless. To tell the truth, he was not so helpless at all. Indeed, his attacks on Parliament, not to mention his end of year speeches, made him famous in all circles. He didn't have too much trouble saying things that nobody else dared to say without a moment's hesitation. He was elected President in 1978 – an unfortunate year for Italy – and actually, once he moved into the Quirinale, he transformed his Presidency into one of less talk, more action. Italians adored Pertini's animated and folkloristic gesticulations. He was an honest, fresh and old-school Socialist. He aptly represented an Italy that reacts and doesn't stand still. Despite his age, he was really on the ball."

"Have we ever had any good politicians?"

"Of course, we've had some really great ones. High-quality statesmen like De Gasperi, Saragat, La Malfa, Vanoni and many others, and above all Einaudi, a true political giant."

"I thought Einaudi was a publisher…"

My daughter always managed to break my flow with the simplest yet most disarming comments.

"That was his son Giulio," I corrected her. "While his father Luigi is rightly considered the father of the Italian Republic."

"Can't we talk about *living* politicians, *current* politicians?"

"Elena," I answered with the smile of a patient father. "It's only by understanding who came first that we can decide who is worth coming after. Otherwise, what form of comparison do we have? Moreover, it helps us understand why young people go in and out of fashion among politicians.

As I was saying, Einaudi was a staunch monarchist but a vocal anti-fascist, who reluctantly accepted his appointment as second President of Italy from Alcide De Gasperi, another sacred prodigy who always dressed in grey, never cracked a smile and who nobody could ever make laugh. A straight-up Piedmontese, Einaudi didn't want to be President; he was elected thanks to the manoeuvres of those who opposed the appointment of Count Sforza. Sforza was a Don Juan and priest-hating republican who would have wreaked even more chaos on the Quirinale than the provisional Head of State, Enrico De Nicola, who had thrown numerous tantrums over the previous two years. To make matters worse, De Nicola didn't want to leave, and it took him time to understand that nobody wanted him in the most coveted seat in Italy."

"It sounds like *Game of Thrones*," Elena murmured fascinated. "But was Count Sforza really so depraved?"

"Probably not, but he certainly wasn't too popular among the left-wing Christian Democrats of the time, and they were the ones who pulled the strings in that little theatre.

During this time, communication between the parties was maintained by Giulio Andreotti – remember that name – who was young at the time and Undersecretary of the Prime Minister. He was also the messenger selected to communicate with Count Sforza, who was already waiting with his inauguration speech when Einaudi was chosen over him."

"I bet he was happy. Was Count Sforza handsome?"

"The count went on a rampage! He had a charming physical appearance. I suppose he looked a bit like Gabriele D'Annunzio. Elegant with a white goatee, the polite and eloquent manner of the career diplomat that he was. Quite the opposite of the shy and reserved Einaudi, who also had a limp."

"He was lame?"

"Yes, the world-renowned economist, Rome correspondent for *The Economist* and former Governor of the Bank of Italy shared this characteristic with the American president Franklin Delano Roosevelt. But in any case, he marched straight ahead when it came to applying drastic economic measures, necessary to restore an Italy on the brink of economic collapse after the Second World War. I guess you could say that he found his feet quickly, excuse the pun." I took a deep breath. The history of Italian politics was beginning to come to life, despite my pun, which Elena ignored.

"So, he was a hardass? Like Thatcher?"

"Not really. Let's just say that the two shared a certain economic liberalism, but they came from different perspectives. Thatcher was openly inspired by Von Hayek, winner of the Nobel Prize for Economics, and was very much against state intervention in the system of production. In contrast, Einaudi was more open and liberalist, more inclined towards the classical dictates of Keynes, of whom Von Hayek was a harsh critic.

In any case, the two leaders operated in very different times. The exhausted post-war Italy was by no means comparable to the battered England that the Iron Lady took over in the late 1970s."

"Sorry, *babbo*, but I still don't get how this can help me understand today's politics, how and who to vote for!"

This was the rain on my parade, accompanied by the worry of a teenager. I went on undeterred.

"We're almost there, now you'll see. We're at the dawn of modern Italian politics, and factions are already forming within one party, the Christian Democrats. Turncoats have appeared – those people who in theory should have voted as per directives from above, but who change their mind at the last minute, thereby sabotaging their bosses' plans. This still happens a lot today. Einaudi's election as Head of State is a small-scale representation of this. And to put it more simply, a classic example of the typical scheming in politics that still goes on today across the world. On the one hand, there was De Nicola desperately clinging to office and promising important positions to those who supported him. This tactic is still used today.

On the other hand, there were groups that pushed the interests of others – especially economic interests – to put forward their own candidate or allow somebody to rise who would not rock the boat. All this to make sure that the opponents chose a person who, I wouldn't say supported but at least, didn't hinder their aims. After all, politics is nothing more than preventing opponents from doing their part. De Gasperi took over an Italy on the brink of economic collapse and had to ask for money from the USA. We were in such bad shape that he even had to borrow a coat from a friend so as not to make a bad impression at the White House, since his was so threadbare and unpresentable."

Elena looked at me incredulously. I nodded in confirmation and continued.

"Disaster happened from 1953 onwards, a period when the Christian Democrats no longer had their huge parliamentary majority of five years earlier. To ensure a government, a colourful and heterogeneous coalition was formed, made up of Christian Democrats, Social Democrats and Liberals. A real delicate balance of different parties."

"They all sound the same to me," Elena said with a half yawn. I decided to use shock therapy to awaken her interest.

"Have you ever heard of the *legge truffa* – the scam law?"

Her astonished look indicated that she hadn't. I continued enthusiastically. "We often hear about it every time somebody in power tries to change not so much how we vote, but how the votes collected will be interpreted. What many forget is that it actually existed, put into effect by De Gasperi and his colleagues to prevent an ailing Italy from falling into a chaos of ungovernability where the communists, always knocking at the door, finally took over. This law reformed the electoral law for election to the Chamber of Deputies; it modified the proportional system by introducing a *superbonus* for the coalition which would obtain at-large the absolute majority of votes. Imagine how the Left reacted at the time, mindful of how a similar law – the Acerbo law put forward by Mussolini – had allowed Fascism to rise to power thirty years earlier."

"But how does the Chamber of Deputies differ to Parliament? And how do members get elected?"

"One thing at a time. Parliament is made up of two chambers: the Chamber of Deputies and the Senate of the Republic, each of which has the same powers. In fact, it's known as perfect bicameralism. A mixed system is now used to vote for their representatives: 232 deputies and 116 senators are elected in single-member constituencies with a first-past-the-post system by which the candidate with the most votes wins. The remaining candidates are elected by proportional representation, adding the votes taken by the multi-member constituencies.

In total, there are eighteen deputies and senators elected in overseas constituencies that represent Italians who live abroad like me. The parties can stand for election alone or in a coalition, which must be the same across all of Italy, however. A coalition presents single candidates in single-member constituencies."

My son passed by at that moment.

"Coalitions? Are you talking about *Star Wars* or *Transformers?*"

"Stop right there!" I tried in vain. "Let's see if you know as much about politics as you know about cinema, instead of being a wise guy."

"I have to go and study with Giuseppe!" was the reply as he closed the front door.

"Anyway, we were saying..." I continued. "Ah yes, the mixed system with complete separation and thresholds..."

"...with photon beams!" added my witty teenager.

"Don't you start now! One of you is enough! I was saying... thresholds: it's three percent for single parties and ten percent for coalitions, which can't take advantage of the votes of parties that have not exceeded the one percent threshold. If a party fails to reach three percent and is part of a coalition, the votes are given to the main party in that alliance. The candidate elected in a first-past-the-post constituency remains, even if his party is excluded from the proportional distribution."

Elena looked at me with undisguised admiration.

"But how do you remember all this stuff?"

I showed her the Google page opened just before on my mobile phone. Cervantes himself said that honesty is the best policy, bearing in mind that he wrote his *Don Quixote* when he was in jail for irregularities as a tax collector. Reassured that her father was not a genius, Elena took courage. "But does the proportional system work? Bicameralism can't be that perfect, given the mess that the Italian government is always in."

"No, isn't," I admitted, "It only works as long as people keep their promises to voters. The problem is that often that's not possible. Do you remember the famous saying: you can't do politics with ethics? Well, the reason is that principles remain as long as they don't cost too much. A shrewd politician is on the *right side* until he has to go to the *last-minute right side*."

She looked at me in disgust. "And you call that being capable?"

"Maybe not, but it's being *shrewd*, that is, being able to understand what it takes to govern, because without governability, that is, an agreement between parties, there is no State."

"It's all a bit disgusting though!" snapped my daughter.

"Be careful not to judge too quickly. There are two types of people in politics: those who do it and those who take advantage of it."

"My classmate Chiara says that everybody takes advantage of it, no exceptions," she sighed.

I joined her sigh.

I feared that everything was more difficult than expected.

"I'm sorry that Chiara thinks that way, but it's not true. That would be like saying that all students copy during a Greek test if most of the class gets a good grade. Some may have copied, but many may not have."

Elena didn't seem convinced at all.

"Can you really name any honest politicians today?"

Her tone was clearly defiant.

"I can name some, but first, I'd like to finish talking about Saragat, La Malfa and Vanoni," I said, rearranging some papers at random. "Einaudi, as I told you, managed to bring a wave of well-being to Italy and De Gasperi managed to control an increasingly belligerent and pro-Soviet left by creating a government in which Liberals, Republicans and Social Democrats were allies."

"Why was everybody afraid of the Communists? After all, it's not such a bad idea to share everything, especially the means of production for the wellbeing of everybody!"

"To be honest, it was not them who were afraid of Communism; it was the United States. They couldn't allow a government that was friendly with the Russians or they might lose that aircraft carrier called Italy moored in the Mediterranean, which was so strategically placed next to Eastern countries at a time of Soviet hegemony. The famous Marshall Plan, which helped Italy financially, was done on the condition that we did not fall into Soviet hands. Vanoni was an excellent finance minister.

He believed in a stable currency that favoured savings, thereby creating a thriving free trade economy in the long run, without too much state intervention."

"And those on the left didn't agree?" she asked me.

"The far-left, as it was then, believed that the State should intervene on everything, level out everything. The moderate and enlightened Left of the time saw Giuseppe Saragat as its symbol. He was a man of great political acumen, highly respected by all sides, and he did not disappoint expectations. He was a charismatic President and a skilled politician who left a lasting mark, especially when in '47 he took a piece of the left from Togliatti's Communist Party and founded the Democratic Socialist Party. They kept in balance that shaky, and sometimes bizarre, Italy wounded by the struggles between parties in the post-war period of real misery."

"You've given me the history of Italy, Dad, but now I have to go and study; otherwise, I'll have to skip Zumba later."

And with that, she ran off, with the agility of people who do a lot of sport.

I thought of Einaudi who, albeit lame, first dragged and then made Italy run, while I was short of breath, recovering from a first exchange from which I came out battered.

Less history, I promised myself aloud.

Less history... yeah.

3. DIRTY LAUNDRY

"We forgot about La Malfa the other day!" I said entering my daughter's room.

"I just took a break," she replied as if to apologise for the fact that her Latin vocabulary book rested peacefully in the sunlight coming through the window.

"I'm interested in the mafia. Pietro says there's a lot of mafia in politics!"

I laughed disrespectfully. "Ugo La Malfa, not the mafia!"

"Oh no, Dad. I've already done two hours of history this morning!"

"I'll be brief, I promise..."

"You talk like a politician," she said abruptly.

"And like a politician, I'll keep my promise!" I proclaimed as I sat down on a very uncomfortable white pouffe.

"La Malfa has nothing to do with the mafia, but he does have to do with understanding Italian politics, Italian politics done well.

He was a proponent of content rather than alignments that others defended, or even worse, advanced. In fact, he declared that instead of squabbling over who to entrust in government, we should see what needs to be done, and then to achieve it, accept help from anybody who offers – even if they're communists – and put them to the test."

"That's brave!" my daughter said. "That reminds me a lot of the concept of realpolitik that we just studied."

"That's right. La Malfa was a pragmatist and identified the Red Scare not in Enrico Berlinguer, head of the Italian Communist Party, but in his sponsor, the Soviet Union, as it was then known. La Malfa also clearly understood that Berlinguer didn't want to become Moscow's puppet, and by involving him in the government, he would give the Italian Communists an opportunity to free themselves from Moscow."

"Dad," she interrupted me. "All these parties confused me the other day. I wanted to ask you to explain what Republicans wanted, what goals Liberals had, why Fascists were still around with the name MSI and so on."

I repositioned myself on the damned pouffe. It would take more than a year to explain half of what she was asking.

"I could make you a list with parties and manifestos, past and present, but I think it would be pretty useless.

And even looking on the internet, you'd find so much material that it would even drive that brainiac Plato crazy."

Elena's face turned from worried to terrified, like when the teacher tells the class at the end of the lesson, "Just one more thing…"

"So…" I continued, "I'll provide you with a quick and useful method that few people know and that will give you a quick idea of what Tom really promises and what Dick really thinks in politics."

This time her attention piqued.

"What is it?" she asked anxiously.

"Twitter!" was my reply.

A moment of panic: familiarity with Instagram didn't make Twitter any more pleasant to a young web surfer. I continued undaunted. "On Twitter – politicians' favourite social media platform – everybody is limited to just a few lines, and it's become one of the most popular ways to communicate with the masses. This forced economy of expression prevents politicians from hiding behind too many words and turns of phrase."

She looked at me like a cat looking at a reflection of the wristwatch on the floor: why does it move?

"If they exaggerate, people stop following them," I pointed out. "In about 280 characters, you have to express your thoughts clearly and simply. And those who really know how to use it – look at Trump in America, for example – write lots of personal comments, which reveal a lot about their character and stance."

"Can you also post videos?"

"Yes, although they're also limited at the moment to just 140 seconds."

Her face lit up with a smile. She really liked the fact that there were videos.

"Nice trick, Dad. Very clever. Do you have many followers?"

I smiled pleased. "I'd say yes, but I've never really tweeted that much." I repositioned myself once again on that bloody pouffe. "See, Elena, social media hasn't changed how politics is done, but it has certainly made politics more transparent in some ways. The days of hiding behind statements that were lexical nightmares are over, as are the days when somebody could stop a news story with a simple phone call to the editor of his friend's newspaper. Today you might be able to fill a hole on the internet, but then an even bigger one opens a little further on. Everything is news."

"But now there's also fake news!"

"True, but like all phenomena that appear on the internet, reactions are quick. Sooner or later, we'll learn to fight that too. Once it took years to stamp out a bad habit; now, a few megabytes later, things settle down thanks to the people's network."

"A people's network that the Five Star Movement are leading."

She said this in the tone of an experienced political scientist.

"That's also true, but remember that in politics, as in nature, nothing is created; it's just discovered and used."

In the meantime, I began to hate that pouffe more and more.

"Have you heard of Brown's Law?"

I asked the question as I hovered in mid-air so as not to fall off the pouffe.

"Which Brown?"

"The one who said: The best way to be successful in politics is to find a crowd that is going somewhere and stand in front of them."

Elena laughed, shaking her head.

"If you think about it, Grillo and co. have found their audience and got them engaged, with their movement," I added.

"Do you like Grillo?" she asked treacherously.

"Beppe Grillo was a devastatingly good comedian. I never missed a show. And he always attacked everything and everybody, most of the time with great intelligence and just as much energy. He's the kind of person you either hug or choke, as somebody said. I've always rated him."

"You didn't answer, Dad..."

This time I fell off the pouffe. "As a politician, he's shrewd, very cunning. He says true and intelligent things, but he's playing with fire. The consensus of people online is fickle and volatile."

I managed to sit respectably on the carpet, my back leaning against the wardrobe.

"And what does Berlusconi play with?" she reiterated.

"Berlusconi doesn't play with anything. He's a very skilled enchanter during election campaigns, a great communicator and certainly one of the most able people in politics at the moment. Not only does he know Italy well, but also the Italian people. He's always been very sensitive to the concerns of entrepreneurs, but equally to the concerns of housewives. He also has incredible people at his side like Gianni Letta who doesn't mince his words with him, his true guardian angel. It's not for nothing that Berlusconi himself described Letta as *a gift from God to Italy*."

"Guardian angel, in what sense?"

"Do you know how I describe my job role when asked? Usually, they call me the director's right-hand man, but I prefer to say that *I protect the director from what he wants*. Sometimes what somebody wants is not necessarily what works best or achieves the best results."

"Do you like Berlusconi or don't you?"

I approached the question in the fatherliest way possible.

"Have you ever heard me say *I like* anybody?"

"You say that about Mum," she replied at double speed, with a sly twinkle in her eye.

"Elena! What does that have to do with this? Let's not digress. That's completely different. I like all people who *do*. I can't stand people who criticise others and never put themselves in the firing line. I find inaction very dangerous: Dante rightly put the slothful in Hell."

"In the Vestibule!" the *Liceo Classico* pupil corrected me. "Since they'd never decided to act and always followed the strongest, they didn't even deserve the real Hell."

"They had tremendous punishment inflicted on them," I interrupted. "Chasing an aimless banner naked, attacked by hornets and flies that tortured them, blood sucked by flesh-eating worms."

"Don't remind me!" she sighed. "The teacher asked me about it in an oral exam and one of my friends almost vomited when I explained it. But what good has Berlusconi done?"

"Berlusconi has done so many things. He certainly hasn't stood still with his hands in his pockets. He's streamlined the bureaucratic machine, removed conscription, introduced a ban on smoking in public places, improved the law on self-defence, regulated immigration and much more."

"Pietro says that he's been put on trial several times."

"And who hasn't in Italy! If you want to create problems for somebody, you make a complaint and he's guilty *a priori*, poor thing."

Elena looked at me puzzled.

"But what do you think?"

"To tell you the truth, it worries me more that there are some judges who spend more time doing politics than investigations. When the judicial system is used for political purposes – and this happens not just in Italy – there's clearly something wrong: the various state powers must remain separate, but it's not always easy."

I stretched out my sore legs.

"When Berlusconi was in government, an interesting and almost paradoxical thing happened: the left-wing opposition, which had been practically non-existent before, stood united and decisively. Until recently, the left in Italy were always ready to blame each other. They were like a group of students on a class trip. Berlusconi arrived and suddenly they marched like cadets in a military academy, with shiny shoes and white gloves."

She laughed heartily. She was well aware of the comparison.

"Speaking of white gloves, what are *mani pulite* – clean hands? A friend of mine mentioned it yesterday, but I didn't understand what it meant."

She sat down on the carpet next to me.

"That was a bright-tailed comet of many hopes in Italy, especially for the young people of the time. Unfortunately, it ended up as a self-igniting meteor in an absolute vacuum."

I paused for a moment.

"It all started in 1992 when a prominent Socialist, who aimed to become the mayor of Milan, was arrested after being caught red-handed pocketing a bribe. Shortly thereafter, the investigation, led by Judge Antonio di Pietro, expanded dramatically, uncovering a wicked system of pervasive corruption at all levels. Out of everybody, the Northern League benefitted most from this deluge of arrests and trials of famous figures. *Rome steals!* was their favourite slogan, which Umberto Bossi flaunted with the force of sheer populism."

She interrupted me. "Pietro says that he'll vote for Bossi, the only clean politician."

My laugh was almost exaggerated this time.

"Tell Pietro that Bossi is not having a great time today. Better keep looking around, poor boy."

She looked at me suspiciously and irritably.

"*Babbo...* you're always so diplomatic. You almost seem to like them all!"

"That's not true, but I don't want to influence you. I prefer you to find material on your own and then make up your own mind about a given person, rather than get influenced by what others tell you. The advantage these days is how easy it is to obtain information from various sources. The important thing is that the sources are authoritative and not bar chatter!"

I managed to get a smile out of her.

"How do you know if the sources are authoritative?"

"If it's a State organisation or spokesperson, it's credible. For example, the *Official Gazette of the Italian Republic* is the official source of knowledge for all regulations in force in Italy. They disseminate, inform and formalise legislative texts, public and private acts that must be accessed with confidence by the Italian people. You can also find company charters, procedural documents, official notifications of sentences and so on, and being published by the Ministry of Justice…"

"… they should be accurate!" she completed my sentence laughing.

"Hopefully…" I murmured, with a hint of concern.

"But regardless of everything, do you like the Northern League?" she asked brazenly.

"Elena, stop reducing everything to a like as if it were Facebook. Political and social reality is far more complicated and can't be reduced to a raised blue thumb on social media. I can like a movement, league or party. Sometimes the problem is the faces that represent it, or the long hands of those who push from the shadows that worries me. I've always been wary of people who lash out too much against everything and everybody, calling everybody thieves. As the saying goes: the guilty dog barks the loudest."

"Quit *hounding* me and let's get back to business, Dad!" she said laughing.

"Brava, very funny! Seriously though, populism is one of the aspects of politics that scares me the most because inciting crowds often has tragic consequences, with many innocent people trampled for nothing. Reason speaks; ignorance and injustice scream. And in Italy, instead of improving arguments to defend valid ideas, everybody tends to raise their voices. If everybody screams, nobody hears the real reason: conscience, ethics. Unfortunately, when they hear the ringing of their conscience, many people pretend that it's not theirs, just as they do in church during mass."

Elena giggled in amusement.

"The conscience doesn't scream," I continued, "It whispers softly because it loves you, even when it's telling you things that hurt and you don't want to hear them. If you scream, I move away, but if you whisper, I move closer to hear you better."

I said these last words softly and Elena spontaneously moved closer to me without even realising it, but it didn't last long. She understood the trick. I continued from where I had deviated.

"The *Mani Pulite* wind turned into a real hurricane. Numerous suicides were added to the many arrests and incarcerations, including that of Raul Gardini, the well-known president of the huge Ferruzzi-Montedison food and chemicals conglomerate. Many politicians ran for cover to save what could be saved and the Biondi decree was issued, which in fact cancelled out various crimes of *Tangentopoli* – Bribesville – as this great investigation was called.

55

This was such a serious gesture that Di Pietro and his team declared on TV that they couldn't continue, given that the decree had actually stopped them, but reiterated that it would have been ethically right to continue. Film-style events followed with incredible twists, such as attempts to make Di Pietro look corrupt, an assassination attempt on a judge foiled by a whisker and various other tricks. Even though it was proved that he was innocent, Di Pietro resigned anyway, and people took to the streets, violently protesting the corrupt government, headed by Giuliano Amato of the Socialist Party. At that time, Berlusconi declared that the resignation of the team of judges left a bad taste in his mouth, and I agree. The government worked for less than a year due to so many scandals. Then Amato was followed by Ciampi, an independent, who lasted a little over a year. Ciampi was replaced by Berlusconi, who remained in office for only eight months, when Dini, another independent, took over. He didn't last long either."

"Worse than *Game of Thrones*," she said in amazement.

"The investigation spared nobody at all, so much so that the then powerful leader of the Socialist Party, Bettino Craxi, had to take refuge in Tunisia due to the whole debacle. Soon after, what is known as the *First Republic* ended in utter disgrace.

The human cost of washing that dirty laundry in public was high, including several deaths, but there were also financial costs, since corruption causes tangible damage to a country.

Just think about the fact that a job that should cost one hundred euros ends up costing three times as much so as to feed the whole chain of bribes required along the way, not to mention the politician who manages to build a bridge where there is no river, perhaps using an engineer who designs it as if it were a dam."

My daughter stared at me for a long time. "And then what happened?"

"Various governments followed one another, and *Mani Pulite* was not only forgotten, but also singled out as an operation in which judges had been overzealous. Di Pietro later hung up his gown, founded a party and became a minister twice. And so, ended an era that had promised so much, especially to young people. In any case, it was a real peaceful revolution of civil society, as some called it."

"How sad though!" Elena sighed.

"Yes, even if in many ways I see it as one of the few historical moments in Italy where nobody was good or bad and the judges themselves who were the main perpetrators of *Mani Pulite* were, in turn, stained with something that we Italians are experts in: a surplus of attention-seeking behaviour. Giovanni Falcone, the great anti-mafia judge killed by a car bomb, said that *we must be careful not to confuse politics with criminal justice.* If we do, Italy, the alleged cradle of law, risks becoming its tomb. And despite having enormous power, in addition to high respect from all, Falcone was very modest. He never took advantage of it."

57

"What do you mean by attention-seeking?"

"Unfortunately, we Italians are a bit narcissistic, actually very narcissistic. As a nation who loves their image as creators of taste, we often look arrogantly at others who *have no style*, as if appearance were the most important thing. Just look at how we do TV dramas: in the American ones, when a police officer chases somebody, they sweat, get dirty, get injured, while in our series, it's like our law enforcement officers work alongside hairdressers; after a breath-taking chase, they never have a hair out of place! All beautiful and sexy, without a mark on their uniforms and the smiles of *Pasta del Capitano*."

"Whose pasta?"

"Forget it, it's a popular toothpaste."

"True, they all look like models," she added.

I kept trying to forget these images taken from a '70s photo story book that our TV keeps producing. Shows with handsome policemen in perfectly ironed uniforms, even after they've been crawling on the ground.

Many of our politicians love to appear on TV, even if they have nothing to say. They find fertile ground on certain TV programmes that leave them freewheeling. And sometimes you don't understand a thing, not just what they say, but what year we're in.

"I don't watch TV, you know that," she pointed out.

"You and your peers might not, but my generation and a

couple of generations before do, too much. When the Five Star Movement began to break out of the darkness, Beppe Grillo forbade them from going on TV, arguing that talkshows lose votes. The principle was right, but in Italy if you're not present, they speak for you. It's not for nothing that we're one of the few countries in the world where tacit consent is even officially sanctioned."

"What do you mean?" she asked curiously.

"It means that in Italy not expressing your opinion has even become legal with the Madia law. So, in many cases, if you don't respond to a request within a certain number of days, it's considered to have been granted. I should note that the law has good intentions, that is, to streamline the bureaucratic machine. In fact, it's only applicable to Public Administration and those who manage it, so it excludes private individuals. In any case, it's absurd that a law has been made to remedy the fact that Public Administration has a really long time to respond or even *loses* the request presented, or worse, it gets lost in not responding."

"Do you mean that if I ask you something and you don't answer me within ten minutes, you said yes?"

"Brava! Nice try!" I said, accompanying my words with an affectionate gesture. "Anyway, yes, that's it: today, you see Grillo supporters much more. It's impossible to stay away from the small screen in a country like ours, where you go to a bar on your new motorbike even if you live one hundred metres away.

It's mandatory to be *seen* at every opportunity."

"No, you've always worked *behind* the camera…"

"…and behind the typewriter too! No, I don't like to be seen, except when strictly necessary."

"So, you wouldn't go on TV?"

"I've been on it. I've spoken in public several times, and when I presented some of my books. Anyway, there are a lot of people who speak well, but speaking well is not enough. You need to have something to say. Better to say one thing and say it well, rather than drown people in a sea of porkies."

She laughed heartily, her green eyes amused by that funny word. "You say that not all politicians are corrupt, but I think its because they're good at washing their dirty laundry at home."

"I can't see a politician doing laundry by hand. He wouldn't even know how to turn the washing machine on."

Her gaze became stern. Better fix that quickly, I thought, using the sweetest tone possible. "I believe that, especially in politics, we get the people who we deserve at that moment, either by accident or because somebody voted that way. Believe me, there are more smart people in politics than you can imagine, but there are also bad apples and knuckleheads, as in all walks of life where you find human beings."

I sighed slightly.

"Sometimes our rubbish is recycled in Parliament, but we created it ourselves."

4. YOUTH

"*Babbo,* have you ever written poetry?"

My daughter stood there at the door of the study, her gaze resembling Cicero ready to address the Senate.

Before I could reply, she had already gone around the desk, placing down her Latin book, more than 700 pages entitled *Men and Voices of Ancient Rome.* Practically a threat.

"Have you written any?" she pressed.

"It depends…" I answered anxiously.

"On what? If there's moonlight?"

Her mocking smile betrayed something sly, the typical expression of somebody who knows something when the other person doesn't.

"Come on. Spit it out!" I said raising my hands.

Triumphantly, she adjusted her dress and sat down beside me.

"Do you know who the *Neoterics* were?"

She was staring at me, but her eyes were smiling.

"I doubt they were gladiators, so I suppose that their weapon was a stylus instead of a gladius," I replied.

"Almost, *babbo*... almost."

She opened the book to page 264, and there they were, written in the red of Imperial Rome.

She was dying to explain it to me, so I pretended to have tired eyes.

"I can hardly see that. Why don't you tell me about them?"

In a semi-serious professorial tone, she began.

"The *Noeterics*, or *poetae novi*, were part of a group of poets who strongly despised tradition and focused everything on poetry. They rejected any political activity, which was unthinkable at that time because they were wealthy, young people for whom politics was practically a family obligation."

I admitted my ignorance and seized the opportunity.

"I see that young people's lack of interest in politics was already a thing back in 65 BC," I said slowly.

"The only difference being that their days were occupied with quite a different kind of tablet."

I exaggeratedly gestured towards the iPad.

"Very funny!" she said in the tone of a teacher who wants to laugh but at the same time has to keep her students in line.

"Did you know that very few people in my class are interested in politics? Even those who call themselves Northern League supporters or whatever don't really care."

"In the past, politics was made by young people saying *I don't care!* and to great effect."

She looked at me as if I had blasphemed.

"That's right," I added firmly. "In the Fascist period under Mussolini, they used the poet Gabriele D'Annunzio to coin various slogans for their propaganda that appealed directly to young people, including *I don't care!*

You can still see some of the slogans around Italy, graffitied on walls or embroidered on pennants in museums. They're relics of an ideology that shocked Italy for twenty years until 1946. Fascism understood immediately that indoctrinating young people was essential to creating secure support in the future, and all education – at home and at school – was based on heroic concepts, which young minds could easily grasp. Mussolini even had his biography written especially for children, citing personal episodes of epic heroism – whether true or made up – which encouraged children to give importance to camaraderie, physicality and discipline. Songs praising youth were also used, which emphasised the warrior and fearless spirit of the young. The most famous is actually called *Youth*. It was written years earlier as a school anthem, but then became the anthem of the newly emerging Fascist Party."

"But what did the Fascists want?" she asked me, spitting out the word as if it were poison.

"All totalitarian regimes, whether right or left, only want one thing: control, with blind and faithful obedience to the dictator or the party. In actual fact, even in communist countries such as Stalin's Russia, it was the party and the people who commanded in theory, but it was only Stalin who gave the orders in practice. The Fascists in Italy theorised the supremacy of the Italic race, affirmed that there was only one truth – that of the party – and that everybody must serve the good of the party and the supreme leader."

"And what did the Communists want? And how did they differ from the Socialists?"

"Exactly the same things, just with different colours."

"Are you kidding, Dad?"

"Of course I am. Reducing apparently similar positions to different ideologies is dangerous, but that's what you'll hear from people we'd define as apathetic. And when discussing politics, these people often have strong arguments, not in terms of content but in terms of appearance, and as we know, looks can be deceiving. To put it simply, socialism and communism arose as the same thing. Once, they were used interchangeably. Both wanted a social and economic system opposed to capitalism, with the disappearance of private property and social and economic equality through the cooperation of all. Even today, the term cooperative is practically synonymous with communist activities, that is, activities done by people – members – whose economic and non-economic benefits are redistributed. There are various types of cooperative societies and they are distinguished from limited companies by their declared purpose: for a cooperative, the aim is to guarantee that its members work or reap the fruits of their work, such as Co-op, the supermarket."

"Mum doesn't go to the Co-op often. She says she can't find the *stracchino* cheese that I like there."

My daughter always brought me back down to earth with the reality of bread and cheese.

"I'll remember that the next time I shop. Let's say, however, that the distinction *a posteriori* made by the theorists of the left was that socialism is the utopian, theoretical version, while communism represents its practical, scientific application, which leads to the dictatorship of the proletariat."

"Dictatorship? But they're communists! I'm still a bit confused, especially by all those names you mentioned yesterday: Christian Democrats, Socialists, Social Democrats, *Missini*..."

"Okay," I interrupted her. "Then, let's sort things out and see if I can provide you with a simple and logical reference for everything."

Elena beamed with sudden composure.

"As I told you days ago, if you want to see various currents of thought in detail, movements and so on, Wikipedia has excellent summaries at the beginning of the definition, which then develop in an orderly fashion."

"Yes, I've read bits here and there, but there's a lot of things to take in! All sorts of stuff!"

I repositioned myself in the chair.

"The term stuff has always reminded me of Giovanni Verga and his tragic novel of the same name, *La roba*, published in English as *Property*. The desperate attachment to goods that are never enough. A disposition of mind that makes us blind and deaf to anything but work, aimed at producing even more stuff. In the end, we can't take anything with us when we die, not even by killing our own ducks and chickens as the protagonist does in Verga's novel."

"Dad, what's that about chickens?"

I looked at her as if she could read my thoughts.

"You whispered *ducks and chickens...*"

"Ah yes, I was thinking about how certain parties are actually chickens disguised as ducks, more flamboyant feathers but in the end... anyway, where were we? The parties, yes. In any case, I'd advise you to take a quick look on the internet, even if what Wikipedia can't tell you is the perception that these parties and currents of thought have created in Italians."

"*Perception* in what sense?"

"Let's see. In Italy, if you mention the word *Socialists* to people of my generation, they automatically don't think of people who want to transform society into an equal place for all citizens economically, socially and legally. And they don't even think of a party that was founded at the end of the 19th century, the first real party in Italy, given that at the time there was only one left and one historical right. When they hear the word *Socialists*, the first thing that comes to their mind – and mine – is thieves."

She jumped in her chair.

"Do you remember *Tangentopoli* and *Mani Pulite*? It all started with a prominent Socialist, Mario Chiesa, who was arrested after an entrepreneur asked for help from the police. He was fed up with paying bribes to be the supplier of a nursing home, the Trivulzio, which was headed by Chiesa, who Bettino Craxi, the head of the Socialists at the time, described as an *isolated rogue*. Craxi, however, soon ended up isolated himself even in company, since almost a large number of Socialists were investigated, tried and convicted, to some degree. And I say 'almost' because there were also many good people among their ranks, but they were all labelled thieves," I sighed disconsolately. "Beppe Grillo, whose criticisms of the corrupt Socialists was the selling point of his satire, had said it almost ten years earlier when he imitated

Craxi's heir apparent, Martelli, during a famous prime-time RAI broadcast. During a trip to China, he asked his boss: *Listen, is it true that there's a billion people here and they're all socialists? Yes, why?* Craxi answered. *Well, if they're all socialists, who do they steal from?* Amid the general laughter, an icy phone call from the powerful Craxi caused the most astute comedian in Italy to be thrown off RAI, and we've seen where shrewdness leads. A few years later, the Trivulzio kicked out Chiesa because he spent some time behind bars and then blurted out everything."

"And what was the Trivulzio exactly?"

"The Trivulzio was a nursing home for the less well-off elderly in Milan. It was a public institute, that is, the people who ran it were appointed by the regional government. So, you can just imagine how angry people were when it turned out that these poor old men and women were being fed a spoonful of soup less to feed Dr. Chiesa! All hell broke loose and the Socialist Party soon went down like a lead balloon."

"Grillo had predicted it many years before!" she exclaimed.

"I told you he's good…" I whispered.

"If only he yelled a little less!" she completed my sentence with a wink.

"The Christian Democrats, on the other hand, were founded after the war, under the name Christian Democracy," I resumed.

"What a clever name! And they were allowed to call themselves that?"

"Absolutely! Yes, a clever name, just like Forza Italia, right? But let's go in order and we'll get there. At exactly the same time, or thereabouts, we find the Republican Party, the Liberal Party, the Communist Party and the Italian Social Movement, known as MSI. In fact, their followers were called *Missini.*"

"And in what sense were they social?"

"They were the remnant of what remained of the Fascists in Italy. The Fascist Party was outlawed by none other than the Constitution."

I thought it was time to offer some written validation.

"Hang on..." I added casually.

I opened the computer and found what I was looking for.

"Here, listen to this: XII transitory and final provision of the Italian Constitution: The reorganisation, in any form, of the dissolved Fascist party is prohibited."

"But it says transitory!"

"Yes, but in typical Italian style, despite being inserted between the transitional and final provisions, it's of a permanent nature and of an equal value to that of the other provisions of the Constitution."

"Are you sure?"

"Yes, of course," I smiled reassuring her, "It's not me saying that; it's the official Law."

"But the MSI was created and they were Fascists."

"Former Fascists, and in any case, it was perfectly legal. There was only a five-year ban on anybody who had held office in the old regime voting or being elected."

"But what's worse? Fascism or Communism?"

I loved how at that age everything came down to simple, better-worse, sick-salty positions and if you've got no idea what the latter means in modern-day slang, then you're reading the wrong book. You're definitely out of touch.

"Let's put it this way, and excuse the simplicity," I said with false modesty. "But we can say that both of them resolve the complaints of those who join."

She looked at me with the hope of somebody with one number left on their lottery ticket to win the jackpot.

"Both take away the trouble of thinking from their followers, since it's the state, the party or the big boss who thinks of everything. It's no longer the state serving the citizen, but the citizen serving the state, or the common good if we want to dress our usual chicken like a peacock."

Her smooth face broke into a big smile.

"When you say it like that, it sounds a bit scary."

"Unfortunately, if we have to sum it all up in a few words, that's the history. Speaking of history, let's see who else arrived on the political scene in Italy after the First World War."

I grabbed a piece of paper and pencil to help me a little. "There were three parties: Catholic, Fascist and Communist, founded at the end of 1918, and they were always known as *whites, blacks* and *reds*. After the fall of Fascism, the mass parties were the Christian Democrats, or DC, and the Italian Communist Party, the PC. The PC had great influence because they were the main supporter of the Partisan Resistance and they became the second party in Italy – the first on the left – relegating the Italian Socialist Party, the PSI, to the background. And so, for more than forty years, the Italian Communists were the only opposition to the hegemony of the Christian Democrats, which at times joined forces with the Socialist Party to govern."

I caught my breath. Elena didn't seem too bored.

"Forty years is a long time. How did the Christian Democrats rule for so long when our government changes all the time nowadays?" she asked all in one breath.

"The simplest answer is that everybody was afraid of the Communists, the red terror. Italy was a special case really. In other countries around us like Germany, England and France, the left was more moderate and indigenous."

"Indigenous in what sense?"

"The Italian Communists were openly receiving aid from the Soviet Communist Party and at the time Russia did everything as long as they were in government."

"And why didn't they succeed? The Russians are powerful!"

"It was thanks to the most Communist of all in Italy, who was also their leader: Enrico Berlinguer."

"That doesn't make sense!"

"Yes, it does, because Berlinguer understood that an Italy under Russian hegemony would be a disaster, pure and simple. Their model would not work for our poor peninsula. One of the all-Italian characteristics of our country's politics is that the leading person – the most influential person at that time – conditions everybody. We are not a people who raise the banner of *principle*; rather, we love and lazily follow the leader who makes us feel most comfortable. Italians have a short memory and Ugo Ojetti – one of the greatest Italian journalists ever and one of the founders of the Italian Encyclopedia – said that Italy is a country of contemporaries, without ancestors or posterity. Therefore, without memory. Keep in mind that he had seen many things first-hand, since he served in the First World War."

"Without memory and without principles, we're in bad shape." She said it with a hint of bitterness.

I tried to alleviate that pain.

"Keep in mind that having few memories allows us to be happier. We live in the moment more, and sometimes being too attached to principles makes us stubborn and dull."

What I was saying didn't sound too convincing, so I decided to resume talking about parties.

"However, since the 1950s, the DC has never had enough votes to form a government on its own, given that the Italian electoral system was exclusively proportional, so much so that in the 1990s this system allowed small secular parties…"

"Secular, as in non-religious?" she interrupted me.

"…not just unlinked to a religious denomination, but democratic parties that follow neither Catholic nor socialist ideology. For example, the Italian Liberal Party, which emerged from pre-fascist liberalism or the Italian Socialist Democratic Party, formed from a piece of PSI and the Republican Party. Without them, there was no government in Parliament. The term *secular*, when referring to Italian politics, has a broader spectrum of meaning with different shades."

She yawned, trying to mask it, but she couldn't.

"Sorry, *babbo*, but I don't think politics is very exciting. All these colours just seem a bit… grey."

"On the contrary," I replied. "There are twists and turns and extremely colourful figures throughout history. My favourite in that respect was Marco Pannella. When he was around, things got really animated!"

"What do you mean?"

"Pannella was the founder of the Radical Party in the 1950s, which came from a split in the far-left wing of the Liberals at that time. He was a figure with a thousand battles and endless speeches, but they were full of passion and interesting things. A great brain."

"Shrewd?" she added quickly. My little girl was starting to chew on politics.

"Probably yes, if you consider shrewd as being able to understand where the popular wind will blow tomorrow and prepare the sails in advance. He also contributed to huge innovations, such as the abortion law, the abolition of nuclear power and many others. He was a friend of the Dalai Lama and Jean Paul Sartre admired him. He had private meetings with Pope John Paul II and even Pope Francis called him from time to time. He pushed prison reform to improve the conditions of prisoners and, in protest against the corrupt system, he helped the porn star Ilona Staller become elected as a deputy. He was tried several times, for the most disparate charges, and he remains perhaps the most eclectic and interesting figure on the Italian political scene. When he died in 2016, the national and international press described him as *a hero of civil rights and freedoms*. In short, a true legend."

"You really liked him, Dad!"

"I've always admired people who believe in their own battles, but who are also capable of admitting that yesterday's ideas no longer work and we must move with the times.

Pannella was one of the first environmentalists, when there was still no talk of the environment in politics, and a very compassionate person who fervently defended the right to equality for women, homosexuals and transsexuals. Unfortunately, many remember him most for his famous hunger and thirst strikes and for the countless hours that he spoke on air on radical radio."

Elena got up from her chair, carrying the 700-page Latin book with her.

"Speaking of countless hours, I have to go and finish this chapter for tomorrow. You know how it is with us young people!"

She gave me a big smile.

"It was precisely with young people…" I added, "…that Pannella knew how to speak. Especially with young people."

"You mean *to* young people?" she corrected me.

"No, no, *with* young people. Listening to them and understanding what they needed, then becoming a megaphone that amplified what they thought and needed, making it heard by those who governed the country."

This last statement earnt me a nice peck on the cheek.

"You always listen to me, *babbo,* even if you talked a lot today. Now I understand how the poor deputies sitting in Parliament listening to Pannella for hours felt!"

Laughing, she walked away quickly, avoiding a playful slap from me.

"Off you go then. Otherwise, you'll be late and your mum will tell us off for getting lost in incomprehensible chatter."

"I'll tell her that we were doing politics!"

And she disappeared into the corridor laughing amused.

Blessed youth, I thought.

5. LEAVES

The leopard-print rucksack was thrown down heavily next to my bag, which had a British Airways label still attached to the handle.

"*Babbo!*"

Elena climbed into my arms like she did when she was a child. But today, as a woman, she almost knocked me down.

"*Stellina!*"

Cristina looked at us with the patience of a mother who understands that the relationship between father and daughter will always be special.

"Get to the table, children, and wash your hands first! Schools and airports have the same kinds of germs."

At the table we laughed and joked as always, but there was a question in the air that I smelt strongly like the scent of pesto on pasta.

"I'll tag along when you go for coffee if you want."

I received her signal loud and clear. There were questions that demanded answers when yours truly needed caffeine.

The sun was out and after coffee we decided to take a walk along the river. Spring was still very far away, but there were already signs that winter was starting to give way.

"I'm discussing politics more in class, but my classmates are too extreme!" she began suddenly.

The student extremism of my high school years flashed before me. The sit-ins and school assemblies between red scarves and black jumpers that ended in fights; in other parts of Italy, they ended even worse: with Molotov cocktails and barricades.

"In what sense are they extremists?" I asked.

"They say that it's all useless, that nothing changes anyway and that politicians are all rotten."

I stopped under an oak tree on the riverbank, which was stubbornly refusing to lose all its leaves, as if surrendering to autumn were too big a shame for a centuries-old tree.

Looking at the bare branches of that practically naked giant, I asked her what she saw.

"Bare branches…" she answered curiously.

"Anything else?" I insisted.

"A few leaves."

"Brava! Take a good look at those leaves that are hanging on, that don't want to leave the tree."

"Maybe it's the tree that won't let them go," she retorted.

I smiled. She was starting to see things from different points of view. I went on, feeling encouraged.

"Politics is like this tree: we only ever notice those who give up and cause damage, who impoverish the structure, and we forget those who hang on until the end. We ignore that society – the tree – sometimes abandons its children to the fickle wind of dangerous ideas, without making any effort to help them. However, let's not forget that when these leaves fall to the ground, they help ensure that the tree feeds even as they rot. Everything is necessary in nature – even rot – as long as the humus produced nourishes young branches."

"Pietro asked me to name an honest politician. After I told him what Bossi did, he told me that everybody steals a lot."

"There he goes, the cynic! Anyway, that's fine. If you want names, let's do names. He claims to be a Northern League supporter, right? Tell him that Roberto Maroni has so far shown himself to be straight-up. He was also an excellent Home Secretary in difficult times. If he carries on like that, he'll remain a very strong figure as others just make fools of themselves."

"Pietro likes Matteo Salvini," she added.

"Salvini is very intelligent, but I don't know enough about him. He understands his electorate perfectly. He speaks simply and clearly. I hope he doesn't disappoint either."

"Chiara told me that she's on the left, but her mother is smitten with Vittorio Sgarbi. What party is Sgarbi in?"

"The political Sgarbi ran as mayor of Pesaro for the Communist Party, joined the Youth of the Monarchist Party, became municipal councillor for the Socialist Party, was later elected deputy with the Liberals, ended up in Forza Italia, later flirted with Pannella's Radicals, moved on to the House of Freedoms – centre-right – then to the Union – centre-left – with Prodi, founded the Party of the Revolution and now has his own party called the Italian Renaissance."

I said it all in one breath.

"Another clever name!" she answered amazed.

"Yes, but in keeping with his character. He loves that artistic period and he knows a lot about art for sure."

"And what do I tell Chiara. Who is on the left? Who on the left is honest?"

She looked at me with a mixture of apprehension.

"There are people. For example, Pier Luigi Bersani is respected and has a reputation for being honest, as does Piero Fassino."

A leaf fell slowly from a branch. I caught it.

"The important thing is that we don't take everything we read in the newspapers or hear on TV at face value."

"Why not?"

I leaned on the fence that protected the embankment. The sun was really pleasant. Too bad that our conversation wasn't bathed in the same warmth.

"It's difficult or impossible to find a newspaper or TV channel that is not biased."

"Do politicians pay for the newspapers?"

"It's a bit more complicated than that. Do you know how newspapers survive? Where the money to publish comes from?"

"From the cost of the newspaper, the subscriptions."

"Unfortunately, that's only a small part. The bulk comes from advertising and the same goes for TV."

"Sorry, Dad, but what's that got to do with politicians? Companies want to advertise to sell more products!"

"True, but many companies receive subsidies and funding, even laws in favour, from politicians. The *big* company bond – and I mean really big – with the political world is inseparable, and it happens all over the world.

If a company needs to resolve an unfavourable situation, for example, an excessive import tax imposed by a foreign country, it turns to the politician to resolve it."

"And what happens to the politician?"

"The company, for example, pays the politician's election campaign expenses, contributes to the party's coffers and so on."

"But that's illegal!"

"It's actually perfectly legal and is governed by a law created on purpose, which came from a referendum twenty years ago, that states parties can no longer receive any public contributions whatsoever, only from private individuals. At the end of 2014, public funding – even election reimbursements – was officially eliminated, giving citizens the choice, as is already the case for religious denominations (the famous eight per thousand) and for non-profit associations (five per thousand). The taxpayer – that is, the citizen who pays taxes – can decide which party the two per thousand of his tax, called the Irpef quota, goes to."

"What if a person doesn't decide?"

"Then it goes to the state, to be part of the public budget."

"So, an entrepreneur or a company can decide who to give that tax money to, right?"

"Quite right."

"But who pays the salaries of deputies and senators?"

I pulled away from the fence, brushing off my jacket.

"Salaries, which in the case of deputies and senators are called *indemnities*, are paid by all taxpayers, through the state.

"Pietro says they get twenty thousand euros a month!"

"No way! Tell Pietro not to talk rubbish! Just go to the Senate website and you'll see that a senator earns five thousand euros a month after taxes and contributions.

Also, keep in mind that by law it's not possible for a deputy to combine their indemnity with any income from public employment other than that covered."

"But they can work privately."

"Yes, of course. They can give advice, but they have to declare it and they pay taxes on it like everybody else. So, if somebody is an entrepreneur, lawyer or freelancer, they can continue to do that job as well as be a deputy or senator, but if they are a lecturer at a state university, a police officer or a civil servant, they must *put on hold* that job until they fulfil what is called a *mandate*."

"But do politicians get discounts? Allowances?"

"Only while they're in office, using strictly personal cards for travel within Italy, by air, rail or sea, including motorways."

Elena looked at me surprised.

A man passed by with a dog enraged at the world: the anger of little ones that we adults sometimes don't understand. We headed home.

"Do you think it's a problem if politicians have two jobs?"

"I'd prefer them just to focus on what they've been elected for, but it's also unthinkable, given the temporary nature of the mandate, that they abandon a career built with years of sacrifice. The problem is more the conflict of interest that can occur."

"What do you mean?" she asked smiling.

"Imagine a member of parliament who is a lawyer and has to go and vote in Parliament on a law that will directly affect one of his clients, how do you think he'll vote?"

Elena sighed deeply.

"He'll vote according to his conscience."

"I hope so too, pet. I really hope so."

She nodded at my shoulder. I noticed a leaf that was clinging desperately.

"You see, there are those who don't give up and want to change their destiny!" I said.

I took it and threw it into the water. It was immediately swept away by the current, whirling around.

"Beautiful destiny!" Elena exclaimed doing a pirouette.

"You never know, maybe it'll help an ant to float!" I said mimicking the gesture of a floundering ant.

We laughed like two little frogs waiting for spring.

6. SUPERMAN

We had moved from the absolute silence of the last take to the excited buzz of the end of the day. The director was still there congratulating me on my beautiful shot, pointing out that my unexpected camera movement was a master stroke. The typical on-set hyperbole.

"You saved the scene, Franz. If you hadn't had followed that actress when she moved, this would have been a disaster! You've got an amazing instinct for anticipating movement!" He said it with the type of emphasis seen in films after the hero has saved the world.

He hugged me excitedly, still drunk with the emotion of the just finished scene. I timidly returned his hug. I still haven't got used to these 'darling hugs', as the Brits call them. The actress approached to thank me, secretly worried that her improvisation had caused problems. Around me, my assistants shook with desperation, anxious to disassemble the camera and go home.

"Let's move away, so my guys can pack up," I said to the small crowd that had come to say goodbye.

After the set goodbyes, I retrieved my mobile phone and turned it on. In addition to the typical notifications of new Twitter followers (but why do these people want to follow *me?*), several messages appeared on WhatsApp.

My agent was asking if I was available for a chat about an upcoming job, my son Enrico had sent me a CNN clip about Trump's latest misdeed and Elena was asking me to call her.

When my children write to me, it's as if I can hear them speak. I can sense their voice on the keypad.

I called her immediately.

"Hi, *piccina*," I replied to her "*Babbo!*"

I haven't told you yet why she often calls me this, alternating it with Dad and Daddy. The custom began when I was shooting a film in Tuscany and Elena came to visit me on the set for a few days along with her brother and mother. These visits were quite rare as most of my work tends to take place in very distant locations that most would define as exotic paradises, but for those who make films, are actually logistical nightmares. It was her who began to call me *babbo* with a marked Tuscan accent after hearing the people on the set say to her: "You really love your *babbo*, don't you, *piccina?*" and those two words with the beautiful accent of Dante's region made an immediate impression on us.

"*Piccina*, what is it?" I said emphasising the Tuscan fall in intonation for comic effect, sensing her nervousness.

"I had an argument with Pietro today in class. He asked me if you were right-wing or left-wing. I replied that you are neither, but he made fun of me saying that we're all either right or left."

Despite the noise of people disassembling the set, I could clearly hear this obsessive left-right. My brain tossed like the heads of spectators at a tennis match.

"*Babbo...* are you on the left? Pietro told me that he's on the right and that from what I've told him about our discussions, he says that you're on the left."

Blessed youth! I thought, as I gave the boys directions on how to put away my work kit, but making sure that Elena wouldn't catch me, like a magician on stage talking to the audience and at the same time setting up the trick without anyone noticing.

"Tell Pietro that I'm not a left-wing man because those on the left often give left-handed compliments."

A moment of silence, then the scolding came.

"*Babbo*, come on... be serious!"

"Sorry, I just wanted to make you laugh. Tell him that I liked the right, but that lately it's taken a bad direction."

She laughed, both amused and irritated at the same time.

"It's okay if you don't want to answer. It doesn't matter!" she snorted.

"No, come on... I'm just a little tired. I'll be home in an hour. Give me time to sort myself out and I'll call you, okay?"

"Whenever you can... I'll pass you over to Mum who wants to say hello."

Cristina confirmed that Elena was really nervous about the conversation with her classmate. She asked me to calm her down as only a father can do. It's one of those phrases that we parents use, which doesn't mean anything but which offloads the problem onto somebody else.

I arrived home on a cold London evening, but that sort of English cold that can't quite make up its mind, almost polite.

When you accidentally bump into a Brit on the street, they apologise, just like they do when it comes to their country's weather. It makes no sense at all, but they apologise for the weather with beautiful sunny smiles.

When I finished sorting myself out, I called home to Italy and after less than two rings, Elena answered.

"What a coincidence!" I exclaimed surprised.

"No, *babbo*. I knew it was you!"

That should reassure anyone, especially a parent, yet the awareness that she had awaited my call with so much anxiety added a further weight.

I decided to use the most reassuring and warmest tone that I possibly could.

"Let's pick up where we left off. We were talking about how our Pietro flies to different parties like a capricious Peter Pan!"

"Stop your silly puns, *babbo!*"

We laughed. My description of Pietro had broken the ice.

"One thing at a time then. What do you want to know?"

"I don't understand why you have to define yourself as right or left. What's the point? Ideas are ideas, aren't they?"

I took my time.

"Yes and no. Look, it's better for us to take a step back so we can clarify why certain concepts are misrepresented and distorted. In other words, why they are exploited for purposes other than those for which they were created."

"I'm lost..." she murmured.

"How can I put it? The so-called exploitation of others' ideas is a game that has always been played in politics, not just in Italy. Thinkers whose ideas or thoughts, especially their philosophical thoughts – which were not linked to any particular colour or alignment, left or right – have been heavily exploited. I mean, they've been used to support or justify a position that they were absolutely against. We could say that it's a case of history making a summary trial out of philosophy."

"For example?"

"Nietzsche: the nihilist par excellence and the creator of the myth of superman."

"We haven't studied him yet."

"I can imagine... and even studying him, I'm not sure how much you'll understand. There are people who have spent their whole life studying him and have only scratched the surface of his complexity of thought. However, just think that the German philosopher was used by the Nazis to fill their ideological void. They drew heavily on his theories, in no small part thanks to his sister, a fervent Nazi, who transcribed, manipulated and finally published her brother's works after his death." Meanwhile, I could hear Elena tapping the computer keys.

"Here it says that his writings are anti-Semitic and Nazi."

The beauty of the internet, I thought. Franz vs. Google.

"Nietzsche wrote poetically and was a very tormented person. He suffered from debilitating migraines since childhood. In the second half of his life, he suffered from a psychiatric illness and had severe depression. His health took a progressive cognitive decline, ending in profound dementia with stroke. There's both witness and factual evidence that he was not a Nazi at all, even overlooking that he was a strong supporter of individualism – exactly the opposite of what Nazism proposed, that is, the sacrifice of the individual for the common good that is embodied by the dictator.

The Nazis distorted Nietzsche's famous concept of super-man, *übermensch* in German, manipulating it into believing that it referred to the Aryan race and the German people."

"Superman as in the superhero?" she asked sarcastically.

"We better not go into that or we'll be here until tomorrow. It's not really that complicated, even though his writings were, and that's why they're so controversial. In any case, there are two important facts that save him. First, it was Nietzsche him-self who declared in one of his extreme *Madness Letters*, sent from Italy: *All anti-Semites ought to be shot*, a provocation, but at the same time an omen, given what was about to happen in Europe with Hitler. Second, it was also Nietzsche who broke off his friendship with Wagner, the famous musician, precisely because he was fed up with the latter's anti-Semitism. Among other things, it should be noted that two of Nietzsche's best friends were Jews."

Elena kept banging away on the keys.

"Here it says that in any case he is associated with Nazism."

"And so he always will be, unfortunately," I added, "Now that doubt will remain, thanks to the damage done by his sister."

"I would never do such a thing to my brother!"

I chuckled, then said in a fake German accent: "Enrico could easily be interpreted. Sometimes you don't understand a thing when he writes!"

"Come on, Dad!" she wailed in defence of her brother.

"You know that I'm joking!"

"Not funny!" she said with a fake pout, but perhaps it wasn't so fake.

"Enrico doesn't like politics either, but he'll still go and vote despite the fact that many of his friends won't."

"I know, I'm working on it," I answered slowly.

"To please him?"

"No, because you must understand that not voting is dangerous. Even when there's nothing you like or that convinces you, not voting is giving the vote to those you don't want."

"Not voting is not voting, *babbo*. It means abstaining."

"Sure, but by doing so, the preference could go to whoever you don't want. Imagine there are two candidates and ten voters. Three vote for one and four vote for the other. If the other three decide not to vote, who gets elected?"

"The one who got four votes."

"That's right, and it might just be the person that you like least of all. Voting is important, although sometimes you have to hold your nose, as somebody said."

"They could make voting compulsory then."

"That's not possible in Italy. It would go against our fundamental democratic principle of freedom of expression written in our Constitution, the famous article 48:

All citizens, male and female, who have attained their majority, are voters. The vote is personal and equal, free and secret."

"So, it's free, not mandatory," she said quietly.

"Yes, but remember that Article 48 continues by stating: *The exercise thereof is a civic duty.* So voting is a must, even though it's not mandatory."

"Are there any countries where voting is compulsory?"

"Oh yes, they do exist: Australia, Argentina, Brazil, Bolivia, Greece and many others, even Belgium."

"And what if you don't vote?"

"You're punished."

"But don't these countries also have freedom of expression as a fundamental right?"

"Yes, but they force people to exercise it. Well, to tell the truth, they require everybody to show up at the polling station. Then whatever a person does when they're alone with the ballot in front of them is their business. The actual vote is secret; you could just draw a flower on the ballot if you wanted."

She laughed at the thought.

"But will they arrest you if you don't show up?"

"As far as I know, in Belgium they rarely take action if you decide not to vote, even if the law itself is quite strict. In Australia, I know they give you a fine, but it's not very much. In Greece, it's written in the constitution that you have to vote, but there's no law that establishes a penalty if you don't.

What they should do is make the voting process simpler and more accessible to everybody, while maintaining necessary security. Being able to vote online would be ideal for young people and would save millions of euros in election expenses."

"Like the school gradebook."

"Even safer than that I would hope! Another measure would be to introduce an option that gives voters the possibility of rejecting all candidates in the running, an option called *none*."

"Are you joking? What do you mean?"

"Ask yourself why many of Enrico's friends don't vote? Because they think that their vote will make no difference, that the candidates on the list are all corrupt and there's no way to express this. So, with an option like none, you could reject all the candidates and they would have to do it all over again."

"I like that idea!"

"I think such a proposal would panic the political world, even if that nihilist Nietzsche would like it very much."

"Why has politics in Italy become so complicated?"

"It's not really, but Italians, they are becoming more and more complicated with each passing day. Blaming politics is easier than admitting your own shortcomings. First of all, that of not being informed and believing everything that is served up by the media, without bothering to check other sources, even those that go against our beliefs."

"You also watch FOX News, which many people say is biased."

"Of course I watch it. I'm interested in knowing how the news is interpreted, or misrepresented, by different voices. If you don't know when somebody is manipulating the truth, you accept news that is clearly fake as real news."

"Fake news."

"Exactly! We also tend to confuse two concepts that are similar in appearance but actually far apart from each other: complex and complicated. A mechanism can be complex when it's made up of many parts that perform different functions, but is not necessarily complicated. On the other hand, complicated is something that, through our own ignorance, appears obscure when it's actually us who doesn't understand it out of sheer laziness. Nature, for example, is complex but not complicated. In politics, a situation is complicated when two different positions refuse to find common ground, blame each other, ignore possible solutions out of a matter of principle or total stupidity, turn the problem into a superhuman effort."

"They need Superman!"

"You only have to start reading Nietzsche to discover that the philosopher considered the person closest to superman to be somebody like Goethe, rather than a Hercules! Nietzsche describes the superman as somebody who builds his own values, who is independent, who doesn't follow trends but creates them.

A selfish and somewhat narcissistic person, capable of harming others for a greater good."

"Like a politician..." she whispered sadly.

"Or like all of us," I replied with a smile. "Nietzsche actually used the concept of superman to make us understand how we might evolve. And if we don't like the picture that he paints, there's an alternative: working more and together with others for the most noble common goal, which is to improve the life of everybody, instead of continuing to complain that everything is complicated and rotten in Italy."

She yawned, hiding it with a little cough.

"It's true, *babbo*. Even Machiavelli wrote that in the last chapter of *The Prince*, urging people to take the initiative and fight, confident that the value of Italians is far from dead."

"Talking of death, I'm actually dying of sleep! I'm sorry but I'm off to bed. We start early tomorrow morning. I have to get up at five!"

"No sweat. You're Superman!"

She always managed to make me laugh.

"I'm Batman rather, as tomorrow I'll have to use tricks to run at full speed, and I don't mean drugs! Goodnight, *stellina*.

"Goodnight, Daddy."

7. SAND

It wasn't a good night's sleep at all. I never tend to sleep much – four hours a night on average since as long as I can remember, just like my mother – but when I'm abroad, the weight of distance from my family is really hard to bear and it keeps me even more awake. Usually, I start writing my next book, but this time I had already started three and they were all left there with just a few pages written and then the paper left stubbornly white, pale with insomnia. Just two more days, I kept repeating to myself, and then I fly home.

It was more than forty degrees outside and yellow sand covered the glass panels on my hotel room window, despite being on the seventh floor. The effect was that of a perennial sunset, a gold with tinges of red that, if you went out fearlessly into the street, you'd find are an intense yellow, like steel before melting orange. I visited the gym, as deserted as the barren plateau that surrounds all of Abu Dhabi. I observed the machines with practically new weights and cables. Chrome-plated cathedrals in a desert of parquet.

I looked at them like they look at a dead Terminator in the movies – a mass of steel that could come to life at any moment – but in my case, they remained still. I just couldn't recover from a week of shooting scene after scene in the desert. Sand and heat penetrated my every pore.

On a bench in the corner, I glimpsed the *Corriere della Sera* newspaper, probably left by some Italian customer, perhaps one of the people I had met shortly before in the lift. They had the important air of people who do business with the sheikhs and seemed disturbed by my presence in shorts and T-shirt, my trainers an intense blue like the shirts of the Italian national football team. I lazily leafed through the *usual news*, as Italians would say, and chanced upon a cartoon by Giannelli depicting two gentlemen. One was saying: *Grillo's supporters have decided: a suspect can be a prime ministerial candidate.* To which the other gentleman replies: *They're finally starting to get involved in politics.* I smiled to myself, folding the newspaper in half. As I went back to my room, I thought that was certainly a great way to explain to my daughter how you can understand politics with just a few glances. The genius of political cartoonists can mockingly grasp what really lies behind so many incomprehensible speeches: the comic unveils the fanciful. My phone beeps with the trill of WhatsApp, a blessed application that holds together loved ones and friendships, at least in my case. I imagined that Elena had once again read my thoughts.

It often happens that I'm thinking of her and then she writes to me or vice versa: elective affinities.

It was actually my son Enrico.

"Dad, can we talk?"

I called him, thinking it was for the usual IT support he needed from time to time. He's certainly his mother's son!

"Hi, Enrico. Wait until you update your computer again, better than..." He interrupted me. "No, Dad. I'm not calling you just for that. I wanted to know how you were!"

"We eat sand and don't drink wine!" I replied with the emotion of somebody who melts just hearing the voice of the 'piece of my heart', as they say in Naples.

He laughed heartily. "You don't drink, Dad."

"And how are you? Is uni going okay?"

"Yeah, yeah. Everything's fine. Today I spent the day in A&E. Very interesting. Our tutor is amazing."

Enrico is in the third year of a Medicine degree.

He's handsome, tall and intelligent. I always imagine him walking around the hospital with the nurses whispering in fascination as he passes by.

When my children were little and they asked me what I would have liked to be if I hadn't done cinema or been a writer, I answered: surgeon.

"Why surgeon? To save lives?" they insisted.

"Partly!" I replied. "But above all, to take off my mask and stare into the eyes of the nurse next to me and say like George Clooney 'He'll live!', just to see her sigh 'Oh, doctor!' with eyes full of admiration." And everybody laughed like students at the end of a lesson, with Cristina scolding me good-naturedly. Full of enthusiasm, Enrico told me about the latest happenings at university, making me experience his world through the passion of a twenty-year-old who is still not troubled by life's burdens. Then he came to the real reason for the call.

"Have you heard from Elena?"

His tone betrayed something. His baritone voice quivered.

"Not yet," I replied. "I was thinking of calling her right now. Why are you asking? Is there something wrong?"

"No... no..." he lied shamelessly.

"Tell me, Enrico! You're lying through your teeth."

He replied with a long sigh, the sort of sigh that a doctor asks you to do so they can auscultate your lungs.

"I talked to her before and she was a bit nervous. She wants to talk to you, but she said you're never online."

"I'm sorry. I've been in the middle of the desert all week. There was no signal. I'll call her now."

"Dad..."

"What is it, Enrico?"

"Isn't it a bit soon to talk to Elena about politics?"

It wasn't enough that her mother was protesting, now her brother was too. I sat on the bed.

"She's almost eighteen, Enrico. Remember that next year she'll be able to vote!"

"Yes, I know, but the political world isn't pretty."

"Politics is a world like many others and talking about it only helps Elena feel more secure, learn more and not be influenced, not even by me."

"You've never discussed politics with me."

"That's not true. Maybe not explicitly, but we've always discussed the news since you were little, and lately we've been talking a lot about Trump and his Incredible Army of Brancaleone."

"His what?"

"Don't worry about it. Do you understand?"

"Yes, yes, but that's different. That's American politics. In any case, Trump is Trump."

"Politics is politics, even when it's a show like Trump's. Behind the boasts of the American president, there are real and serious issues that are also relevant to our country. The language and the size of the GDP might be different, but the problems stay the same."

"I don't know, Dad. I wouldn't be so sure."

"Do you remember a long time ago when we discussed how the social dynamics of Trump's America might seem different to those of Italy, but can actually be found there too? How populism is an effective transversal control technique at times when people are scared and are constantly kept in a state of renewed fear?"

"Yes, I remember."

"Or the fear of the economic crisis, of immigrants who rape, steal and take away jobs, the repeated threat that political opponents take away your fundamental rights, such as property, security and even family?"

"The same is happening in Germany, Greece and many other countries as well," Enrico added with a light sigh.

"See, Enrico. Same problems. So, don't be fooled by what you see from the outside. The problem inside is global. It's just the size of the scale that is different. When there are repressive totalitarian tendencies, which take away the freedom of speech, the right to study and lead to discrimination based on sex or skin colour, you understand that it must be discussed."

"But do you think it's okay to discuss these things with Elena?" he insisted respectfully.

"If she wants to know more, then why not?"

"How would you explain all these angry populists to her?"

I changed position on the bed, taking my time. Still not happy, I sipped some water from the bottle above the minibar.

"It's more useful to explain the phenomenon rather than who is part of it, so I would start with an analysis that is easy to remember. Populism is founded on a strategy common to all: perception is created and a problem spreads, possibly something that affects everybody personally, such as home burglaries. Immediately afterwards, the urgency of this issue must be felt, so the message is amplified and distributed at every given opportunity. Often, statistics are distorted or sensationalist cases are found, even better if they are threatening. Once this is done, a simple solution is offered, but it can't be *do-it-yourself*; it must be something that only me, the proposed candidate, can solve. I must emphasise that my quality as a leader is required and that others lack the skills or the courage to do so. So, I offer a strong leader with a readymade solution. Once the threat is extinguished, either because it's no longer talked about in the media or because it naturally disappears, I have to immediately find a new one with the same characteristics, even better if it's even more terrifying. And so, citizens – people – are controlled by exasperating and exploiting their fears."

I sipped more water to clear the sand from my throat.

"Then a true government of the people is not possible, since the people can't be *trusted*. That's an easy trap for anyone with a bugbear," Enrico said as I swallowed.

"Exactly!" I replied. "In fact, historically nobody has ever managed to create a government that is truly based on direct action by the people, given that the danger that demagogy will take hold and become a government of summary executions is very real. In politics, there's a tendency to do what you often see in old western movies. The person at a disadvantage throws sand in the other person's eyes and then grabs their gun and fires."

Enrico gave a little laugh, which always sounded profound coming from him. "And you'd know all about sand, Dad. You're an expert at the moment!"

"Bravo Enrico! Laugh at your poor old Tuareg."

He laughed again.

"Come on, Dad. You know I was only messing around."

I decided that it was time to reassure him completely.

"Anyway, tell me whether your sister has complained that my explanations are too technical or too difficult."

"No, no, on the contrary. She seemed enthusiastic."

"And how about you? What do you think of politics?"

"You know how I feel. I don't like anyone at the moment."

"Wipe the sand from your eyes and take a closer look."

"What do you mean?"

"Let's face it. I don't know how much those in power want young people to vote, so the fact that they're averse to politics plays into many politicians' hands as young people are the real voting power. If only you got out there or entered the booth to vote!"

Silence, a typical sign that my words had hit a nerve.

I let him mull it over and took another sip of water before starting up again.

"See, Enrico. Sometimes in politics, people call something a problem when it's actually an advantage."

"What's the point of doing that?"

"It's an old technique: if I'm the first to identify a problem, but also offer a solution — whether it's feasible or not — then I can make that problem that I've created seem like my opponent's problem."

"I still don't understand its purpose."

"Sometimes I create a problem just to then lay it on my opponent and propose myself as the saviour who can resolve it."

I felt his astonishment.

"What a perverse mechanism. Politics sucks," he slowly emphasised.

"These techniques are lent to politics; they're actually old tricks used in advertising and marketing, not to mention other disciplines. I'll give you a non-political example: what do you think a detergent for whites or for colours advertises? What does it want to leverage?"

"That's obvious: that it gives you whiter shirts and sheets, jumpers that no longer fade."

"Are you sure? Nothing else?"

"Let's add underwear too!" he said with a laugh.

"Let's add that as well, but actually, advertising – not just for detergents – relies on one fundamental thing: a sense of guilt. What sort of woman are you if you let your husband go to work in a shirt like that? How will you be able to face your friends if you wear a faded shirt? You have rightly said that they *no longer fade*: so before, they faded and you were useless, but with my new formula, I save both your colours and your respectability. This technique is used not only for detergents, but also for cars: your neighbour has a better car than you, or even better, if you drive this model, you'll be the envy of everybody and women will look at you. This game becomes even more sophisticated when they include famous actors, sports stars or people that everybody admires socially, sees as role models to look up to and imitate; otherwise, you are not *good enough*. As human beings, we constantly need gratification. Look at the importance that most people, especially young people, place in receiving *likes* on social media."

"Speaking of which, Dad, I like that picture of you in a turban that you posted on Instagram! You've got so many likes!"

We laughed together; he had the perfect timing of dry English humour.

"See, Enrico. Politics imitates advertising: it pretends to give you a solution to a problem that it itself has created for you by leveraging your sense of guilt. You'll rarely hear a politician say that things are fine, unless he is in government."

My son seized the opportunity.

"Trump is in charge of the most powerful country in the world, but he keeps saying that things aren't going well. However, people like him precisely because he doesn't behave or speak like other politicians."

"Trump…" I reiterated unperturbed, "…is the cold, hard, unfiltered elementary politician who spreads his thoughts as they come, but his thoughts are just emotions, purely spontaneous. His impulsive comments can and have had serious consequences. People have lost their jobs or been violently attacked or even killed, such as when he announced that he recognised Jerusalem as the capital of Israel."

"But it was already, Dad!"

"Precisely for that reason it was a cynical and irresponsible gesture. He only did it to be able to say to his followers *I keep my promises*, since so far he hasn't kept a single one."

"Let's see what happens with the wall!" chuckled my son.

"Yeah, the wall: a beautiful example of phony demagogy. All immigration experts agree that a wall along the border is useless. There is official US government data showing that illegal immigration is mostly caused by people who stay beyond the term of their visas, not by people who cross the border, who are very few. The wall will not stop the influx of immigrants wrongly perceived as criminals, something that is not true and contradicted by serious statistics, but serves to calm the electoral base loyal to Trump."

"I'm not entirely convinced, Dad."

"So, let's look at it in an even simpler and more immediate way. The problem of immigration from Mexico is not a real problem. All serious economists – all without exception – have publicly stated that immigrants, including illegal ones, are not only beneficial to the economy, but that they don't cost anybody a single cent, especially the Government. So, the problem doesn't exist, but Trump has made it a problem by pushing it with his base like a war cry. He's giving the bloodthirsty crowd something physical, a concrete symbol of perceived discontent, especially that part of the largely ignorant population, who doesn't want to work and claims that the state must support them financially just because they're American citizens. They're unable to hold down a job out of sheer laziness or are unwilling to do menial jobs, even well-paid ones, out of social stigma. Such people consider working as a binman or a waiter, for example, to be beneath them and not good enough for their white *stars and stripes*."

"That's not a nice attitude," he agreed.

"Absolutely not: the reasons lie in the education, or lack thereof, that they've received and the social fabric in which they live, that is, their friends and relatives, who perpetuate false myths and find continuous excuses to justify their state of economic insufficiency. The wall has become the perfect alibi for a person's ignorance and laziness, the worst combination in a human being. The political shrewdness of Trump and others – now and at different periods in history – has created a false danger, which is perceived as real by ignorant people, and legitimised it by unifying those who lack the ability to be self-critical under a single crusade and attributing problems to illegal aliens created by their own incompetence. In any case, Trump is a politician because instead of providing logical arguments based on actual data in response to real difficulties or social conflicts, he just tells stories. Most people don't like logic, but they love jokes."

My throat went completely dry. I looked for another bottle of water.

"That also happens in Italy with immigrants," sighed Enrico, bewildered, taking advantage of my pause.

"Unfortunately, yes," I answered sipping. "But that doesn't mean that there's an immigration problem in Italy; rather, the fear of immigrants is used like the fear of the bogeyman, the black man who takes your children away."

"Okay, Dad. In any case, you have to admit that immigration is a serious problem!"

"Serious, without a doubt. But it can't be resolved with inflammatory statements. You have to listen to people who work in the field and deal with immigrants every day directly: police, doctors and healthcare workers, social workers and so on.

It's a problem that must be addressed in the countries that this diaspora come from. We must collaborate with local governments and help them to contain it."

"But there are wars going on in some countries!" he exclaimed.

"So, we're not talking about economic migrants; we're talking *refugees*, and they must be helped at any cost, until they can return to their country of origin, if possible."

"Elena asked me if you're on the right or on the left."

My instant response was to burst out laughing.

"Right and left have lost their meanings, Enrico. I think we're getting bogged down on archaic terminology that should be laid to rest once and for all. People like labels, but often they become tattoos deformed with age."

"Come on, Dad. That's gross. You know I don't like dermatology!"

I laughed with him and said goodbye. As we were speaking, I had heard message notifications and assumed that it was Elena trying to contact me.

But it was actually the production assistant, telling me that the director was waiting for me at the restaurant, on the right just outside the hotel. I asked if he was right on the right, just to make sure I didn't confuse one direction with the other.

That can happen when you've got sand in your eyes.

8. PULPIT

I've always associated Sundays in Italy with bells and Holy Mass and lately it's also an opportunity to meet ex-schoolmates and friends who I've lost touch with after thirty years living abroad.

This Sunday was no different from any other; the only difference was the homily. The priest who gave the service usually delivered great sermons, but this time – perhaps also due to the awful crackling of the speakers – I just couldn't follow him.

A priest normally prepares his sermon according to the dictates of homiletics, which requires a simple, conversational format, taking the biblical text from the Gospel that was just read as a starting point to talk about today's problems and examining the themes therein.

In politics, many should do the same: examine the topic of the day and develop it, rather than continually pushing second-rate offers like a dishonest fishmonger in the market.

If I ask for a sole, don't give me a dab at all costs.

It might look like a sole, but its taste clearly reveals it for what it is: a poor-quality fish.

And speaking of loaves and fish, this sermon was not only flavourless; it was also poor in content.

It also lacked something as fundamental as salt: pauses.

The priest seemed to be almost in a hurry, adding more concepts in the shortest time possible, forcing those present to do brain acrobatics to decipher the meaning, as well as the words, given the distorted sound.

"Shhh!"

The fur-clad lady stared at me sternly, her finger over her mouth strained in a poorly executed attempt at composure.

I smiled awkwardly and raised my hand in apology.

Her husband who was sitting next to her shook his head, an ambiguous gesture because I wasn't sure if it was in disapproval of me or of his wife turned cop in the aisle seat.

"You're talking to yourself," Cristina whispered, holding back a broader smile.

"Sorry!" I answered chuckling.

The priest took his only pause in preaching from the pulpit, his stern gaze directed towards me, as if the Underworld were about to open beneath my feet.

Elena squeezed close to me, with the protective tenderness typical of a family member in distress, the strength of somebody who won't allow her father to fall from grace.

The monsignor resumed his homily, gesticulating a little more, as if to warn the parishioners of unspeakable punishments if somebody dared to let a fly buzz around again. As if flies could buzz inside a church that was colder than a fridge.

"I'll treat you to a coffee, *babbo!*" Elena said emphatically, taking me by the arm at the exit of the Cathedral. We left Cristina by our house and headed to my favourite bar which, for me – a typical emigrant who had returned home from overseas – made the best coffee in the world.

"Dad, can I ask you a question?" she hinted as we walked.

"Okay, as long as it's not too difficult. I can't think straight before I have my caffeine boost."

While I was sipping my only drug, I took a quick glance at the *Gazzettino*, a newspaper that is very popular in Veneto.

"Do you usually read the paper?" she asked me.

"Was that the question?"

"No, I had another one," she replied politely.

"And what about you? Do you usually read the paper?"

I courageously asked my daughter, trying to distract her from asking another more difficult question than this one, which was already making me feel awkward. Perhaps I should have ordered a double shot of coffee.

"Daddy, I barely have time to study the mountain of homework they give us every day!"

"But if you had time, would you read it?"

I asked moving the newspaper towards her, as if I were dealing cards in a poker game. Elena gave it a fleeting glance.

"I don't understand much of it, especially the political pages. Too many strange names and references."

I looked at the newspaper through the eyes of a teenager. It wasn't actually written with young people in mind.

"Do any of your classmates read the paper?"

She laughed just as a mother does when a child asks why the moon doesn't fall down to earth. At the same time, she pushed the newspaper back towards me with a stilted gesture.

"My male classmates read the pink one about football. Us females prefer YouTube."

The old *Gazzetta* was still popular, I thought, the only paper that speaks the language of youth, between a dribble and an assist.

"To understand politics, you should also read newspapers!" I exclaimed persuasively.

"But I've got you, *babbo*. I don't need newspapers!" she said with an adorably fawning smile.

"Brava! You always get me with that little face!"

I ruffled her hair. She reacted as if I had grabbed a panther by the tail. I withdrew my hand just in time. Her blows could be sweetly ferocious.

We laughed as always, catching the attention of half the bar.

On returning home, I thought about how many of our politicians smiled as they talked, but none came to mind.

As we passed the church, we saw the priest who had celebrated mass coming out in a hurry, a face like thunder. I gave him a little smile, which was blatantly ignored.

"Babbo, you told me that it no longer makes sense to talk about right or left, so why are we still discussing it?"

I hadn't told her anything. Clearly, she had talked about it with Enrico, and I was glad she had done. I took a breath.

"We speak of the left like a bitter aunt who has passed away: few could stand her, but nobody wants to speak ill of her. An aunt who, in any case, leaves her children orphans."

"And the right?"

"That too was orphaned. Once there were people like Giorgio Almirante, head of MSI, a person respected by all sides. Shortly before leaving the party, he told a well-known journalist: *You really think that I'd continue to do politics and lead a party destined to die anyway because one generation goes to the cemetery and another to jail?* This tells you how it was back then in the '80s. The Right was already in trouble."

Elena was speechless.

"Keep in mind that the Right of that time lived anchored to the past. They were nostalgically reluctant to innovate and this imposed and forced nostalgia is precisely the problem with an ideology: by living in the past, you forget about the present and sometimes it backfires."

This thought suddenly invigorated her.

"So, nostalgia as a political weapon doesn't work. Nobody uses it anymore!" she said softly.

"Maybe!" I replied. "Nostalgia starts from the assumption that it was better in the past, but that was only true for a few; for most people, that wasn't the case. Nostalgia is still used as a weapon, not so strikingly, but in a much more subtle way. Trump coined the perfect slogan to serve his populism: *Make America great again.* Clearly, it's nostalgic, a throwback, and it made a huge impression on those ignorant Americans who see the *bygone years* as an ideal time when, according to them, America was *America*, the real, original, Made in USA. Ironic, given that Trump made his fortune with Made in China, from steel to ties... he's one to talk!"

"But he's good at attracting attention. You and Enrico don't miss a single piece of news about him!" she said laughing.

"True," I sighed. "He's just like a child throwing a tantrum in a restaurant: you can't help but notice him. However, the overwhelming trash he comes out with is highly comical. The problem is that his decisions have serious consequences. In any case, he remains a great communicator, but on instinct."

"Not like today's priest in church!" she giggled cheekily.

"Poor man. He did his best!" I added sarcastically.

"So, are priests on the right or on the left? Can they vote? Can they do politics?"

"*Free Church in a Free State.* Have you ever heard that?"

She shook her head.

"It was a phrase coined by a French politician, I think, that was taken up by Cavour the first time he spoke to Parliament. You remember, right? Kingdom of Italy... Rome capital?"

"Yes, yes..." she answered automatically.

"According to Cavour, the Pope should devote himself solely to spiritual power, leaving temporal power to the state, to avoid any problems of coexistence. The Constitution establishes this division as the supreme principle that cannot be changed in any way. Article 7 says that *The State and the Catholic Church are independent and sovereign, each within its own sphere.* So separate."

"So, the Church doesn't intervene in politics?"

At that moment, two nuns passed by.

One was cursing a car that had almost run her over.

"Unfortunately," I continued. "The Church gets dangerously involved in politics, shamelessly."

"For example?"

"For example, declaring how politicians should vote, or asking citizens to abstain from voting, as it did in the 2005 referendum on law 40, the one on artificial reproduction.

In a shrewd political move, Cardinal Ruini didn't say *vote against* – perhaps because every time the clergy had ever suggested voting *no*, the Church had always lost, as in the referendum on divorce and then the one on abortion – but he adopted the phrase of a truly great communicator: *You don't vote on life!* which was to be interpreted as *abstain!*"

"Why was it a shrewd political move?"

"You remember the keywords of politics then!" I exclaimed, embracing her happily. "Shrewd indeed. He knew that a quarter of Italians normally don't vote, so all he needed was another equal amount not to vote, which was aided by the unrelenting heatwave in June, the date when the vote took place. The church focused everything on the human aspect to convince people to vote *no* or to make the referendum fail due to lack of votes. And those in favour of the referendum made the big mistake of positioning themselves as experts in artificial insemination, thereby reducing people's personal emotional doubt to simple cells and test tubes."

"Everyone's a scientist!"

"That's right. Huge mistake. Everybody has their own skills, always remember that. Unfortunately, this is a very Italian problem. We all think that we're Leonardo Da Vinci."

"Enrico says we're a country of national football team coaches!"

"Very true!" I answered laughing with her.

"So, the Church *does* politics."

"The clergy is made up of human beings and man is a political animal, whether of the Church or otherwise, regardless of what he wears."

"But do you think appearance is important when speaking in public?" she asked suddenly.

I stopped abruptly, climbing up a step, assuming the pose of the priest on his pulpit admonishing his parishioners, especially me.

"The habit makes the monk, even in church!"

I repeated gesticulating.

"Dad, be serious. I'm really asking you!"

I composed myself.

"Yes, it's very important: if you observe politicians, they dress in relation to their electorate or to their audience at that moment. Better take off your jacket and tie and roll up the sleeves of your shirt if you want the sympathy of the factory workers. Whether they wear a jacket and tie, shirt or polo shirt, all pay great attention to how they look. Colours also matter, although not as much as in England, where members of the Labour Party often wear red ties, while members of the Conservative Party wear blue. Even Thatcher wore her classic suit in a brilliant blue. In America, red like Trump's tie for Republicans and blue like Hillary Clinton's one-piece suits for Democrats. Here, the Northern League uses *Padania green* and, back in my day, Communist teachers used to come to school in red scarves. In politics, everything is important, not only what you say, but also *how and when*. Sometimes it's strategic, even *where* you say it: a statement made on the fly getting into a car is easier to retract later by stating that it was misreported or out of context, unlike things said at an official press conference. Politicians also often speak indirectly through newspapers, leaking news as accidental scoops when that was actually their plan all along."

"What's the point?" she asked amazed.

"Let's take an example. I'm forced to make a deal with you. Publicly, I can't refuse, but privately, I don't want to, so the ideal situation would be for you to refuse or change your mind. An old trick is to let a reporter know that I'll be with your worst enemy plotting against you in a restaurant at some point. The reporter goes to the scene and takes a picture of me in the company of your opponent, not imagining that I just stopped by to say hello. The photo is published with the following article saying that I'm plotting against you, you change your mind because you don't trust me anymore and I get away scot free."

"But then you're stuck with the other person, my enemy," she reiterated.

"No, because in the meantime, I'd organised a *real* meeting with a friend of yours in the same restaurant and he himself will testify that I only had a meeting with him and the other person only greeted him in passing."

"Diabolical!"

"That's nothing. The history of politics is full of news that was later denied, and it's a true art. It's a theatre of deception that's carried out all over the world, to different levels of sophistication and on different scales. For example, if you and I are head-to-head in the polls, I look for a candidate who can steal votes from you and I encourage him, making him believe that he'll win. Really he just takes votes away from you so I win."

"They think of everything," she murmured as we entered our house, the yellow winter light creating a Caravaggio painting in the hallway of the old building.

"For somebody who wants to win at all costs, there are two ways: give it your all and be the best or make your opponent look the worst. And guess which one is easier?"

"Yeah, but it's unsportsmanlike!"

"It's also anti-democratic if you think about it!" I answered on the fly. "There was a famous example in politics in the 1950s, a guy named Dick Tuck, a master of these dirty games. He was particularly angry with Richard Nixon, who was running for the US presidency at that time. When he was a student, Dick was accidentally commissioned to organise a Nixon rally at the university, but since he supported Nixon's opponent, he booked an auditorium with 4,000 seats, making sure that only about forty students showed up.

When Nixon arrived, he introduced him after a very long speech that casually recalled his failures; then he announced that Nixon would talk about the International Monetary Fund, which he knew he was not at all prepared for."

"Brilliant!"

"He always did terrible things to Nixon, things that were actually pretty funny. Once, he found that bin lorries returning from collection were passing by where Nixon would give an election speech. Immediately, he bought the advertising space on each truck and wrote on it: *Nixon is garbage.*"

Elena laughed heartily. We sat down in the kitchen.

"Politics is not that different from marketing or advertising, given that both base their success, their effectiveness, on one thing in particular: appearance, or rather the perception of name. Voters – those who use their votes – are like consumers when they become customers, that is, when they purchase goods or services. They are persuaded that the product – in this case the candidate – is what they need. So, this product is either presented as something that can't be done without, or negatively as something not up to par, or even as something that will cause great harm."

"You know these things because you worked in advertising," she said with a hint of malice.

I smiled nervously.

"Unfortunately, I've seen things like that, but don't believe that the world of filmmaking or journalism is so different, you know."

"In what sense? Does that also happen in filmmaking?"

I adjusted my glasses.

This made me extremely uncomfortable, but as I said at the beginning of this book, we never lied to our children.

"Even in filmmaking, techniques are used to put your opponent out of business."

"Has it happened to you too?" she asked, her green eyes widening in spontaneous amazement.

"Unfortunately, yes. One of the first agents who represented me took me with her, promising me seas and mountains. Months went by and I was working less and less, and I found it strange because up until that moment I'd been extremely in demand. A friend suggested that I get somebody to call and ask for my availability for a job, and so I did. It turned out that my agent told those who wanted me for a job that I wasn't available, but she had another person who was just as good, indeed a little better, according to her. And he happened to be her boyfriend and I was his most dangerous competitor."

"So, what did you do?"

A bitter smile crossed my face.

"I looked for another agent."

She hugged me.

"You're the best, Dad. The best!"

"Darling, you're biased!"

She jumped out of her chair.

"I'm going out with Mum to get a dress: the habit makes the monk, but also the nun!"

And with that, she ran off.

In the newspaper resting on the sofa, I spotted the outraged statements of well-known celebrities on the recent sexual harassment scandals, many I knew and some I had even worked with. Practice what you preach, I thought.

9. HORSES

It was the first time I rode with Elena and, excuse the rhetoric, but it's been a dream of mine since she was little.

I've always loved horses. For as long as I can remember, I've been obsessed with them: as a kid, they were the only thing I drew. The horse represents everything we should aspire to as human beings. Kindness, strength, elegance, beauty and the ability to be humble but noble at the same time.

When we dismounted, Elena was over the moon.

"How was my galloping?" she asked me, still sweaty, as she removed her back protector.

"A real Amazon!" I replied paternally.

The horse she had rode, Sally – a beautiful half-pony – seemed to laugh with us, while Canova, known as the Professor, followed us pushing me with his head, pleasantly eager to reach the well-deserved food trough. We spent a good half hour tending to them, making sure that their hooves were clean, their coats dry and well brushed, and that their enclosure was straightened out before closing them in the box for the night.

We headed to the car, still basking in the joy of riding.

Despite the cold evening, the country air was truly good for the lungs, including the smell of the stables.

"Does politics deal with the environment?" she asked suddenly.

"Of course, it does. Unfortunately, politicians' attention to the environment depends on the country's economy."

"What do you mean? A lot of people want renewable and green energy, better air and healthy eating."

"Yes, that's right," I replied, "But in the event of an economic crisis, the environment takes a back seat to the fact that people don't have enough to eat. And when the citizen-voter has a rumbling stomach, he can no longer stomach the politicians in charge and sends them packing. The costs involved in producing while respecting the environment are often unpopular; production and distribution processes that are less harmful are almost always more expensive. As long as the economy is fine, politicians have no problem justifying these extra costs or further restrictive measures. But as soon as there is even a hint that families' purse strings will take an unnecessary hit – advocated by a few orthodox environmentalists – then the popular wind changes. However, this perception often stems from wrong information. Look what Trump did with the Paris Agreement!"

"You always bring up Trump!" she snorted sportfully.

"The Paris Agreement is very broad and many countries don't actually adhere to it. But it's the symbol of the will of the whole planet – practically all nations without exception – to do something to save this poor earth. Trump hates it because Obama promoted it so much, and he didn't sign on for two main reasons. First, to show that he was saving jobs in coal mines, the thermonuclear sector and car manufacturing, since, in theory, the Agreement penalises these three sectors. And second, to show everybody that nobody can control the US, especially not France. Obviously, this is not the case, but it was just a gesture to impress his electorate who were hungry for strong signals, which serve no other purpose than to inflate Trump's ego. The truth is that Trump may have unwittingly awakened the green spirit of many Americans who until then were resting on their laurels, confident that enough was being done."

"I was talking about Italy, Dad. Are we really as far behind as Chiara says? She is even a vegetarian."

"Chiara would be better off becoming a vegetarian a little later when she's finished growing. She needs the proteins in meat for development. If you don't overdo it, it doesn't hurt."

"However," I continued, "Italy is among the top countries in the world for renewable energy, behind only Sweden, Germany and other Northern European countries. We're not only doing well, but doing better than many others."

I started the engine. Elena continued pressing me as I reversed. "Chiara says that in Italy we move backwards like crayfish when it comes to the environment."

"I wouldn't be so sure. It may be that we've lost out a bit because of the economic crisis that has gripped Italy since 2006. The government at the time implemented European legislation, which was less strict than Italian legislation. Nonetheless, we are among the top countries in the world for renewable energy. If I'm not mistaken, almost ninety percent of our national energy is renewable."

"Really?" Elena wondered.

"Check on the internet, but I think so."

It began to drizzle, a water that was trying to become snow. The warning light for possible ice on the roads came on. I slowed down and turned on the windscreen wipers.

"Fortunately, the environment is a popular battle that young people feel passionate about. They fear that climate change is a very real and looming danger, but that many politicians underestimate or even deny it, as Trump himself does. Studying the interaction between living beings, including humans, and the environment is the basis of ecology. Unfortunately, it's often exploited by politicians when it suits and then immediately abandoned when it becomes cumbersome and too expensive."

"And when does all this happen?"

"For example, when a motorway is built by deforesting and destroying many square kilometres of land, perhaps a delicate ecosystem containing rare species. The economic interests of factories and transport prevail over the grass of the hare and the puddles of the frogs."

"But that's not fair!" she interrupted me.

"In theory, politics should mediate and find a compromise. Unfortunately, those who helped get the politician elected – perhaps by paying for his election campaign – expect their interests to be protected, while hares and frogs are forgotten about."

"How sad. And can nothing be done?"

"It's indeed possible. Today you've got social media to mobilise the masses within a few hours; in the past, that would have taken days. It's also possible to access traditional media, such as TV and newspapers, more quickly and directly. A tweet or an interesting post can be shared and distributed to many people at great speed, attracting the attention of mainstream media without having to pay exorbitant prices or rely on important connections."

"But you told me long ago that you can't have a direct government of the people because it doesn't take much for the whole thing to blow up, with sudden and unpredictable summary executions."

"I haven't changed my mind, but we'd better change our way home because we can't pass through here."

In front of us a large truck had got stuck between two cars while manoeuvring. There were already several cars in a line and it didn't look like the traffic jam would resolve itself quickly. I turned the car around and resumed both the road and our conversation.

"See, Elena. A good politician serves to guide the people to improve, to guarantee security and governability. Sometimes he has to make decisions that are for the good of everybody but don't please everybody, or make others that are tough in the short term but will do a lot of good in the long run."

"Like a diet!" smiled my teenager.

"That's right. Austerity measures are the typical example. Nobody wants them but they are necessary sometimes."

"But if a politician had one function, what would it be?"

Here we go again, I thought. Typical of today's youth who want to reduce complex concepts to a single phrase, such as memes – images with a sentence that summarises a simple thought – or emojis – those icons and popular smileys on SMS and WhatsApp, where whole sentences can be replaced with little hearts in yellow circles.

"Dad?

"What is it?"

"You were lost in your thoughts."

"Ah yes…" I recovered. "What good is a politician."

My poor brain was now smoking like a car radiator in a traffic jam on a motorway in the middle of summer.

"I'd say that a politician serves to bring people from different positions together to reach a compromise agreement, which allows everybody to work together."

She looked at me satisfied. This time, I had managed to respond with the synthesis that people her age require.

She read my mind.

"You'd be a great politician, Dad."

I laughed as I tried to figure out where to turn.

"You think so? Just because I agree on where to spend the Christmas holidays?"

We laughed as the rain stopped battering the glass.

We stopped at a petrol station to fill up the car with diesel.

"Do you think cars will all become electric?"

"I think so, for one simple reason."

"Which?"

"Now there is the will and the political interest to do so. Before, that was unthinkable. Ever heard of the *Seven Sisters*?"

She shook her head.

"It was the term that Enrico Mattei, a well-known member of parliament at the end of the war, coined when describing a cartel, that is, a group which only protects its own interests at the expense of others. It was made up of the biggest American oil companies of the time, who were even suspected of blocking the development of alternative propulsion systems to the internal combustion engine to protect their interests. Mattei was tasked with fixing *AGIP*, the main Italian oil company, and discovered this agreement between the seven companies, which damaged not only Italy, but the whole world. He managed to make Italy independent from an energy point of view and even formed an alliance with the Shah of Persia, today's Iran. But he disturbed powerful interests and was killed by a bomb while flying in his private plane. The Mattei case was very famous, and others who investigated his death were also killed: the journalist De Mauro, the general of the Carabinieri Della Chiesa, the deputy commissioner Boris Giuliano..."

"A massacre!"

"Yes, it was suspected that even the writer Pasolini was killed because he took an interest in it."

"But why was Mattei killed?"

"Because he upset huge political interests, who had a lot of money – a ton of money – that involved the economies of entire nations, so much so that it's thought that even the CIA was involved."

"A true spy story!"

"Unfortunately, with real deaths. Mattei prevented the Seven Sisters from absorbing the Italian oil industry and created *ENI* which rivalled them, especially in the North African and the Middle Eastern markets. It was the best known and most mysterious political crime of the post-war era."

"Why political?"

"Because it's suspected that those who ruled Italy at the time did not look favourably on the influence that Mattei – considered a communist and in direct contact with Moscow – had on the rest of Parliament. Over the following years, the involvement of the Italian secret services in the case also came out. They were accused of covering up various leads on the instigators and perpetrators of the attack. In short, a truly sordid story."

"And *that* is politics in Italy?" she asked bewildered.

"No, that's the aberration of politics in general, not just in Italy. However, keep in mind that those years were really difficult: from the post-war period up to the 1980s, all kinds of things went on in Italy. In that period, surviving – not just politically – was difficult. There were trade union tensions and continuous strikes, student revolts, environmental protests and rampant and bloody terrorism. Italy was in a terrible state."

"Was there already terrorism?"

"Of course, including the Red Brigades, who kidnapped and killed a beloved and respected politician, Aldo Moro. Those were dreadful years."

We were almost home. I parked and got out the car.

Perhaps I had overdone it.

Elena held the bag containing our helmets and protective gear as if it contained the archive of the Mattei case. An incredible and uncomfortable load for everybody.

"I'll take it!" I said, removing the burden from her.

"So, you can't have clean politics," she said quite disconsolately.

"You can, you can, but you have to choose thoroughbred horses, which give their best and are loyal, and both treat them with respect and demand respect."

I managed to snatch a smile from her.

"You're not happy unless you're mentioning horses, Dad!"

"Horses are always relevant, and if we have thoroughbred animals and we choose the right workhorses… we won't be horsing around!"

"*Babbo!*" she exclaimed in disgust at my joke.

"Okay. Sorry!" I replied, adding the noise that horses make when they snort. She laughed and hit me softly with her riding crop, clicking her tongue – the noise you make with your mouth to make a horse move. She neighed, pawing with her feet, as Cristina opened the door looking at us in horror.

"Leave the horses outside and everything that smells like them too!" she exclaimed peremptorily.

I thought of the muck of Italian political history, of how many people had defended ideals by making them their warhorses, for which they had lost everything, including their lives.

10. ENGINE

I don't use a car much. I prefer motorbikes or walking, although I've always enjoyed driving four wheels.

I know little about mechanics, just enough. But above all, I don't like talking about cars, or even motorbikes.

Don't get me wrong. I'm happy to talk about how beautiful the Jaguar XKR was or passionately argue why I prefer Indian to Harley Davidson. And I must admit that my 1961 Vespa 150GT was the most beautiful *two-wheeler* that I've ever had, and I've had so many bikes!

"Dad?"

"What is it, Elena?"

"You're talking to yourself."

There we go, I thought, Jiminy Cricket has caught me again. Nothing escapes her.

"Your Vespa is beautiful," she added. "It's so *cute!*"

That's how my daughter saw the symbol of young freedom back in my day, a weapon of seduction and independence: *cute!*

We turned into the garage car park, where the chief mechanic – a lovely man named Santino – welcomed us as old friends, although we only saw him on rare occasions like this: annual servicing.

"Are you going to sit in the waiting room or do you prefer to come back later? I'll do it as soon as possible," he said with the calm of somebody who not only knows how to do his job, but is really a lovely person.

"Thanks. If you don't mind, we'll wait," I replied, and we sat down on the faux leather chairs, typical of dealerships and doctors' surgeries.

Elena found a newspaper on her seat and began to leaf through.

"To me, politics is like an algebraic problem, but expressed with numbers from an alien language," she declared. "It's not a solution accessible to homo sapiens."

I caught the slight irony, but decided to venture an answer anyway, unaware of what I'd have to endure shortly thereafter.

"It was Aristotle who stated that man is by nature a political animal, and Aristotle himself who reassured everybody by saying: *If there is a solution, why are you worried? If there is no solution, why are you worried?*"

My daughter looked at me like Giulio Andreotti looked at that glass of water that Bettino Craxi passed him in a debate.

It was the gaze of somebody who has no choice but to trust, even if they're doubtful.

"Dad, I only asked you why I understand practically nothing when it comes to politics in Italy. What does the nemesis of us high school students have to do with it?"

I pointed at a section of engine displayed for ornamental purposes.

"That has something to do with it, because instead of trying to remember a series of notions, we should understand the basic mechanism. Anything this spits out will make sense because we know how its inside works, and if it doesn't make sense, it's because we know what doesn't work and needs to be fixed."

A long pause followed, and I was satisfied that I had done so well. But that feeling didn't last long.

"What is *Rosatellum*?" she asked treacherously.

It reminded me a lot of those sudden questions, fired like a shot, that my teacher used to ask me in high school, interrupting the explanation and making me realise that I was not following. And unfortunately, Elena was right because I was thinking about motorbikes and horsepower.

"Can you explain it to me?"

I looked at the newspaper like the mechanic was probably looking at the oil pan: it needs to be checked, but you're not sure it will end as you hope.

"The *Rosatellum*," I said rolling my tongue over my palate in the hope that somebody would come in and tell me that the car was ready after just five minutes. An unthinkable Formula 1 pitstop time in a normal garage.

My daughter continued to look at me slyly, with an expression used on big occasions: *you don't know!*

I recovered quickly, much to her surprise.

"The *Rosatellum* is the new electoral law passed in October 2017 which will regulate the 2018 elections. It's called *Rosatellum* because there's this trend among politicians to Latinize the name of something or somebody that has to do with a law or a provision. In this case, it was the leader of the PD who proposed it, Ettore Rosato."

She looked at me with an expression that means *you're not getting off so lightly.*

I resumed my uphill struggle.

"I already mentioned this to you a little while ago when we were talking about how you get elected to Parliament."

She straightened her hair, looking at me puzzled.

"Not enough for you?" I asked, starting to sweat in the waiting room, which was as cold as a walk-in fridge.

"I'll help you, Dad. I'll ask you the questions and you respond."

"Okay, detective, would you like to read me my rights first, or perhaps I should start by calling my lawyer?"

"Come on, Dad! So, first question."

I rubbed my hands together and put them on my temples, pretending that I was on a TV quiz with a million-euro prize and needed maximum concentration. Although the stakes were much higher here.

"First question," I repeated.

"Why?" she asked.

"Why what?" I said with undisguised concern.

"Why was a new law needed? Wasn't the previous one good enough? The Matt…"

"…*Mattarellum*, which came much earlier and was actually followed by *Porcellum*, *Italicum* and finally *Rosatellum*. Some were declared partially or totally unconstitutional and therefore another had to be created."

"What ridiculous names! So, the *Rosatellum* is better then?" she asked me amused.

"I don't know if it's better. It favours the formation of coalitions between parties, removes the majority bonus system and limits the number of names on the lists. But its major innovation is probably its *pink quota*, that is, each of the two sexes cannot represent more than sixty percent of the candidates from a list and the leaders of a single party across the country."

"So?"

"So…" I continued, "If there are two seats to be assigned, the candidates on the list must be a man and a woman.

If there are three seats, two men and a woman or two women and a man and so on."

"And does everybody likes this law?"

The PD, Forza Italia, Northern League and one of the other parties – I don't remember which – voted in favour..."

"The Five Star Movement?"

"No, no, on the contrary, they voted against it. So did the Italian Left and two others."

"So, it's better for parties to join forces?"

"Is that your second question?"

"No!" she exhaled, amused at my trepidation.

"It's worthwhile, yes, so that they can back the same candidate in single-member constituencies."

"Here it says that Five Star Movement will not form coalitions."

I nodded, looking desperately towards the garage door.

"I've read that too. In fact, they'll be at a disadvantage, while Renzi's PD would do well to find somebody to team up with on the list."

She looked at the newspaper.

"Why are they talking about three percent?"

"Parties will have to get at least three percent of the votes nationally, but if they're in a coalition, this quota becomes ten percent of the votes. I already explained this to you some time ago. You don't remember anymore? It's called a *threshold*."

"What if they can't?" she asked, ignoring my objection.

"In that case, they can't elect anybody."

"But what will I find on the ballot? They don't explain that here."

I began to think of what Steve McQueen said: *Racing is life. Anything before or after is just waiting.* Santino, where are you?

Unlike Steve McQueen, I had no escape, so I decided to comply.

"You'll see a list of symbols, with pretty ugly designs, and the names of the candidates on the corresponding *closed* list, that is, whose order can't be changed and you can't express a preference for. You can put a mark on the party you find on the ballot and then the vote goes to the party and to the single-member candidate, the name in the biggest font essentially. If instead you put your mark on the single-member candidate, the vote also goes to the party. If it's a coalition, the vote is distributed proportionately among the parties that are part of it. If you've put a mark on a single-member constituency candidate and also on one of his coalition parties, the ballot is still valid. However, remember that you can't put a cross on both a candidate and a symbol to which he is not connected because that will spoil the ballot. Is that clear to you?"

"Not really. But is it possible for two parties to draw?"

"You like this head-to-head, huh? In that case, the party that received the most votes has the majority. The previous law provided for a second ballot, but the constitutional court overturned it."

141

"Is it different in England?"

"The majority share is the same as the UK electoral system and also the US House of Representatives, with single-member constituencies and single-round elections with no second ballot."

"And what about Italians who live abroad like you?"

"There are also seats for Italians who live abroad, divided as follows: Europe, South America, North and Central America, Africa-Asia-Oceania-Antarctica, and they follow the pure proportional system, without thresholds."

"And once the elections are done and the deputies are elected?"

"Officially before starting any government, that is, after the election, the deputies must grant confidence to the government formed by those who won the election. This confidence must come from both chambers."

"What if they don't grant it?"

"Then the President of the Republic dissolves the chambers and calls for new elections. Even deputies and senators, at least a tenth, can put forward a motion of no confidence in the government."

She looked at me disconsolately.

"So, if they don't agree, there's no government. So, do you think it's better to govern or be better represented?"

"What do you mean?" I asked, even though I understood the question very well.

142

"Given that governments in Italy often fall because they can't agree in Parliament, wouldn't it be better if there were a system whereby they *can't* disagree? I don't know if such a system exists but…"

"It does exist. It's called a *dictatorship*, and having to choose between representativeness and governability, the former is better."

"Really?"

"Absolutely yes, every day of the week and twice on Sundays!"

She laughed as she always did, her eyes sparkling.

"You see, our system might have its flaws, but I prefer to have a weak democracy rather than a strong dictatorship."

"Pietro says that dictatorship is the only form of government that would work in Italy."

"I see that our man is back on the right. However, he's telling the truth."

She looked at me in amazement.

"But you just said that…"

"Some people believe that absolutism would be the most efficient form of government if the leader were an *enlightened* guide, meaning that he had a great sense of fairness, justice and moral values, listened to the will of the people and guided them. People like that rarely exist. We're all human and corruptible, especially when we have a lot of power."

"Have there ever been enlightened dictators in modern times?"

I looked at the garage door again. I needed the light from that door so much... if only it would open!

"Not really. Let's say that there have been heads of state with almost absolute power who did good for their country. In particular, I'm thinking of *Sankara* who led the current Burkina Faso for a few years before being assassinated by his deputy. He carried out incredible economic and social reforms, leading the African country from absolute poverty to relative wealth, without any outside help. After he was killed, the country sank back into the corruption and hunger that had plagued it."

I paused, thinking of Sankara who is remembered as the only enlightened African dictator. I heard his story while I was in Angola during the war that tormented that country, but that's another book. You'll have to be patient.

"Another head of state that could be considered an enlightened leader is *Ataturk* in Turkey," I continued. "There, he is revered by many as a saint. Many people are moved just by mentioning his name, as he saved post-war Turkey, which was economically and politically vulnerable to being divided between the British, French and Americans who were eager to control a country that is the bridge to the Middle East. Ataturk created the secularisation of the state and gave the vote to women, making Turkey the powerful and modern nation that it is today.

So powerful, in fact, that when we discuss the Middle Eastern problem, Turkey is rarely mentioned. It's considered more like Europe than the Middle East. Ataturk was the one who insisted that the Turks westernise, even their clothing."

"Let's get back to Italy, Dad. So, the laws before the *Rosatellum* weren't constitutional, right?"

"Some of them weren't, no."

"Can the Constitution be changed?"

"It can be changed, but given the extreme delicacy and importance of such a measure, each change must be approved twice three months later by both chambers, and both votes must result in an absolute majority. It's also possible to change it through a popular referendum, if at least half a million voters or one fifth of the members of a Chamber or five regional councils request it."

"How do you know all this?"

"I studied Law for a few years, then I stopped because I found it hard to study and work at the same time."

"You were working already?"

Her amazement still echoed in the room when good old Santino entered. The car was ready and I was saved.

I paid the bill, thanking the Japanese for building cars that cost so little to maintain.

As I drove, Elena was absorbed by her mobile phone, puffing often and furiously typing replies left, right and centre.

She was clearly agitated.

We stopped at a red light. I felt her shudder with agitation. When the light turned green, she could no longer hold back.

"Michele just wrote on the WhatsApp class group that if the state were run like a business, everything would work better. And he also says that he knows this for a fact because his dad is an entrepreneur."

"Has anyone replied?" I asked, although to tell the truth I already knew the answer.

"Yes, I wrote that businesses can't be used as an example of good governance because they're not in the interest of those who work there, but of the shareholders or the owners."

"And what did Michele say?" I asked timidly.

She frowned. "He wrote that my dad is not an entrepreneur and is not responsible for workers. Therefore, he doesn't understand anything about how businesses work."

I looked at her sideways. She had the threatening look of one of the *Avengers* and I fully understood Cristina when she says, "She really is her father's daughter!"

I ran for cover to save Michele from a horrible death.

"First of all, even if I'm not an entrepreneur, I have employed and continue to employ many people directly, since I'm the one who brings together most of the crew. I personally choose everybody and it's something that I've done with great awareness and responsibility for many years.

I don't just choose the best; often I choose people who I know have problems because they haven't worked in a long time or have troubled situations at home."

Elena brightened.

"That said, when you compare running a business to leading a country – and there's a lot of talk about that these days, given that Trump has made it his signature, despite having gone into serious bankruptcy six times – remember that while a business can fail, a country cannot, absolutely cannot. Look at what was going to happen with Greece, but they didn't allow it. Furthermore, the qualities that make a great political leader are not necessarily the same ones that a great entrepreneur has."

I slowed down to let a delivery van pass that had to turn around.

"Essentially, politics is the process of deciding who gets what, where, why and when. In business, this process is dictated by economic laws, such as supply and demand, and it's rarely possible to create a demand in a market. It's easier to respond to an existing or latent need to obtain a profit, while in politics it's necessary to guarantee public interest more so than private interest. A good example is the management of hospitals: it would be wonderful if they were not at a loss, but if being at a loss means saving lives, then economic loss is justified, although this doesn't mean that waste should be accepted."

"Yes, Dad, but somebody has to pay for those losses!"

"Certainly, and that's why there must be some State activities that generate profit. In doing so, this excess or surplus goes to cover the losses of activities that are fundamental for life or create income with ad hoc taxation. For example, alcohol and cigarettes are not basic survival products, so let's tax them heavily. If people drink and smoke less, the work of hospitals is decreased and we can pay the salaries of doctors, the cost of medicines, structures and equipment needed to save lives. The same goes for schools: education should not be a business, but a fundamental right for everybody and everybody should have access to it, regardless of their social status. I don't think it's right that only those who can afford it should go to university."

I paused and took a deep breath. This was a subject that has always fascinated me, experienced first-hand.

"You see, *stellina*, I believe in meritocracy, that is, with equal opportunities the best should be able to access important positions. And this doesn't mean that only those who are more intelligent are most deserving because even those who work hard must be rewarded, while the slackers must be cast aside. Meritocracy is an ideal form of government, but we must clearly define what we mean by best: those who want to improve themselves and others and have the ability to do so, either because they're intelligent or because they've worked hard to get there."

She looked at me a little bewildered.

"Going back to businesses," she pointed out firmly,

"Especially those that are doing well, I'd say that they are more like tyrannies than democracies, so in theory dictatorship would be better."

This time it was me who laughed.

"No, baby. Private companies are plutocracies, that is, systems governed by those who have assets, money."

"But isn't that the case in many democracies too?" she reiterated undeterred, "For example, in America, to become President, you need millions and millions of dollars."

I sighed looking at her with the tenderness of a father who realises that his children are growing up.

"True, the US is in fact a plutocracy, like many nations now, since people with a lot of money normally have the power to influence those who govern, or even buy their influence."

I parked in the underground car park beneath our apartment.

"The fact that I can drive a car doesn't guarantee that I know how to repair it if it breaks down, modify it to save petrol or improve its performance. So, somebody who leads a company – even a successful one – does not necessarily know how to lead a country, and whoever compares the two lacks ingenuity. This doesn't mean that there are no such people, but even a very good entrepreneur like Berlusconi – and nobody can deny that he's smart – had some conundrums once in government. It's not easy. A government is like an engine, made up of many complex parts.

It takes a good mechanic and a good driver to make it work as it should, and both must play their part."

We got out of the car and walked over to the door.

"Dad…" she said fearfully.

"What is it, *piccina*?"

"If you were in government, what would you do first?"

I laughed heartily, but she looked at me very seriously.

I composed myself.

"I'd resign right away so a truly capable person could take my place."

"You're the best, *babbo*. You'd have my vote!"

She hugged me.

"Can I go to Chiara's party on Saturday evening?"

I turned with an inquiring look.

"Did you vote for me because I'm the best or for purely opportunistic reasons?"

We laughed as we ran up the stairs, competing to see who would reach the top first.

11. EUREKA

"Can you give me an example of opportunism in politics?"

And so, it began. I hadn't even had time to get into the house yet.

"Let me at least catch my breath," I replied, buying some time. "Why are you asking me? Does Pietro come into it by any chance?"

"No, but I want to be prepared if he keeps stressing me out with his theories."

"Is he still on the right?" I grinned.

"He said he was going to vote for the Northern League, but now he's changed his mind. Now he likes the Five Star Movement."

"A big leap, I would say!"

"So, can you tell me an opportunistic trick used in politics nowadays?"

"If you explain to me what you're looking for, that would be useful."

"Pietro still says that there are no dirty tricks and foul play in politics today because everybody knows everything. I'd like something that is used in politics in Italy and that is quite technical and secret."

I sighed exaggeratedly, to give more weight to the *secret* I was about to reveal.

"I'll tell you one that a friend of mine has just told me. He's a journalist, a great expert in Italian politics, as well as a chef and gourmet," I said, "So he really knows how to mix different ingredients to obtain new and tasty results!"

I had just been jogging. I took off my trainers, my knee creaking in a plead with me not to torture it for a while.

"I just need a quick answer, Dad," she said in that peremptory tone that daughters take with their fathers.

I gave in quickly, as fathers often do with their daughters.

"You must have heard that there are many small movements and parties springing up all over the place, right? Like mushrooms in the woods when the sun comes out after the rain."

She nodded her head firmly.

"Well, some are small groups that split from larger formations due to disagreements or rivalries; others arise spontaneously, from somebody's desire to do something that really shakes up the scene, improves it. They're often self-financed, that is, they don't have important sponsors.

Others are initiatives that develop because there's some party (or a specific leader) behind the scenes, encouraging and supporting them, who then brings together votes and consensus when needed. These operations are similar to *fake civic lists*, that is, a leader knows he can't attract a specific group or target so he chooses one that he's confident has a chance. Then, magically, it's announced *this party has made our positions its own…* and then it becomes incorporated. In these cases, however, it's only the bosses who benefit."

"But is that legal?"

"Sure, maybe not quite morally acceptable to some, but perfectly normal. Do you remember what I said the other day about better or worse?"

"Yes, I remember. Quite disgusting, I would say."

"And speaking of disgusting, I need to take a shower. I don't sweat Chanel when I go for a run!"

I managed to take refuge in the bathroom, but from behind the door, I heard her pressing.

"What's the point of civic lists?"

The first thing that occurred to me to reply was: *do they not teach you anything at school?* Instead, I cowardly opted to turn on the water and get in the shower, vowing to brush up quickly on how our electoral system works in detail after drying my hair.

In any case, I would have to use all my creative synthesis skills to show my daughter how it works. A very tiring undertaking, given that – to keep on the topic of water – explaining Italian politics feels like salmon going upstream, with bears lurking.

I never sang in the shower. I don't know if I should, but I've certainly always found that water, or perhaps the bathroom in general, is a great think tank and a source of creative ideas.

I read by chance a while ago that an American researcher at Harvard (and others) discovered that highly creative people all have one trait in common: they're easily distracted. What does that have to do with showering?

If you think about it, with activities like showering, floating in the sea or fishing, you are so relaxed that you loosen the control that you impose on yourself in every-day life, leaving your brain free to wander where you normally don't allow it to go.

As you relax, your mind starts coming up with crazy and different ideas: the classic *eureka* moment of Archimedes who, legend has it, discovered the famous law that regulates fluids when he was in the bathtub.

He announced the discovery by joyously shouting the famous phrase while running naked for Syracuse.

The only time that a light bulb has been switched on in the water without doing harm.

This time, however, creativity was not needed.

It was time to give a simple and quick answer to my daughter on how Italy manoeuvres politics, a continuous game of puzzles and poise, where the things said are just the tip of the iceberg of those left unsaid, and that you'll rarely find written anywhere. I also didn't want to give her a pessimistic idea of politics. Some of her classmates and society in general were already doing that, more than ever today with trolls on the web.

I took a look at the internet – so as not to talk nonsense – and then called in my student, who, seeing the screen open, uttered discouraged: "Dad, I've seen that page on civic lists too!"

Don't say I didn't warn you about young people who already know everything: Google beats Dad once again.

"And what is it that you don't understand?"

She slumped into the chair, the weight of the world on her shoulders.

"I don't understand why they have to complicate the easy and make it difficult."

"By means of the useless," I added. But this time I couldn't even get half a smile from her.

"Listen, Elena, I understand that it's not simple, but *it can't* be simple because our society is becoming increasingly complicated and sophisticated. And a government that doesn't take this into account and doesn't adapt laws and ways to elect its representatives, risks falling into the chaos of those waiting precisely for those contradictions to sink everything, good or bad.

Politics is linked to people – remember what Aristotle said – and we can't have men without there being politics, which arose precisely to regulate relations between them."

"How would you define politics in two words then?"

Here we go again, like all young people looking for a sentence that sums up everything, a funny and quick meme to redistribute on social media.

Elena understood my frustration and met me halfway.

"I don't mean that you can explain everything to me in one sentence, Dad. I know that's not possible, but at least tell me how to understand more."

I took my time. I didn't want to reduce the answer to a joke, not this time.

"I'd say that the best thing to do is to stay informed, not allow certain information to be ignored or distorted. In other words, don't accept that everything that comes from the government is for *our good* or that what you read in the media is really the government's intention. It's always helped me to know as much as possible that has been said on the same topic, even in different periods of history. Machiavelli defined politics as the art of acquiring and maintaining power, while for Karl Marx, it was the organisation of power by one social class to oppress the other. In general, it's defined as the *art of compromise to obtain consensus.*"

"And how would you define it, *babbo*?" she asked interested.

"Good question," I replied. "If you think that Albert Einstein once said that politics is more difficult than physics…"

She looked at me astonished.

"Did he really say that?"

I nodded.

"Politics escapes definitions in the same way that it's difficult to define love or life. When we define it, we've trivialised everything, ignored its complexity."

"But you must understand, Dad, that this alienates us young people. Few people I know of my age will vote, with very few exceptions."

"And why do you think that is?" I ventured, hoping for an unusual response.

"Because nothing changes anyway," was her obvious answer.

"That's where you're wrong. Nothing changes because many, especially young people, think that nothing will change or, worse, they want others to decide for them."

"Come on, Dad. That's the classic old man speech."

I looked at her lovingly.

"Yes… and for many centuries, not much has changed. The old might repeat themselves, but the young have nothing to say."

"*Babbo!* You also always say that *as you mature you end up rotting!*" she exclaimed, adding a sly smile.

Good old Aristotle who taught the tricks of dialectics in such a subtle way to young people, I thought.

"In your opinion, what does it mean *to be mature?*"

"To have experience?" she answered immediately.

"No, it means taking responsibility, being responsible for your actions towards yourself and others. Politicians can also ignore the facts. Look at what's going on in the US as a macroscopic example, but voters, especially young ones, absolutely can't ignore them."

She looked perplexed.

"Let's see. In your opinion, what do all you young people care about most, apart from mobile phones?"

She gave a half smile.

"Holidays?"

I shook my head.

"Instant gratification. That's what young people want today."

I paused, checking the effect that my words had.

"People of your age want instant *likes* as soon as they put a thought on the web. Whether it's a photo or a comment, it doesn't matter. Why do you think selfies are so successful among you young people?"

"Because we're narcissists?"

"Not really. Rather because young people are insecure about many things and the selfie, when uploaded to social media, gives them proof not only that they exist, but that they are *liked,* that is, they get immediate gratification: they become *somebody.* All young people have always sought popularity and for the importance of their presence to be recognised.

Mythology is full of examples of young people who attract attention to reaffirm their existence. And so is history, populated by youthful heroes, driven by the desire to stand out so that their ideals are recognised by all. The same happens nowadays, just at a faster pace and much more extensively. When this desire comes too quickly – perhaps in the wake of populism driven by strong social discontent – it becomes dangerous because this is how unsavoury figures come to power. However, this rarely happens in politics, given that most initiatives are long-term and require the consensus of many, which comes slowly and sometimes not directly."

"What do you mean?"

"For example, I can block your initiative by voting against or ignoring your request to recognise your idea as good. The art of politics in Italy and abroad is based on creating consensus – between parties but also between people – and if the consensus is too immediate, it's sometimes difficult to assess the ramifications and consequences that it could have in time. In politics, haste is a bad adviser, but young people don't like to wait; they want everything immediately, always."

"Is that why us young people don't vote?"

"It certainly contributes, but there's another factor that discourages people from voting: distance. Many young people go to university in cities other than their hometowns and traveling to vote is economically and logistically inconvenient for them.

That's why electronic voting would be an incentive to involve young people in politics."

"We're not in good shape," she said seriously, "But even if that were the case, I think many of my classmates still wouldn't vote."

"I hope that changes, and that our chats will have an impact, not just on clarifying your ideas, but also making you understand that we must not accept that we're told that all politicians are corrupt, that politics is dirty and that voting is useless. It's precisely this rejection of politics that makes it so difficult: we're afraid of what we don't know, but if we know it, we learn to love and respect it."

"Like how you got me to love spiders. They're fascinating if you get to know them."

"Exactly. And understanding how important they are is essential."

She jumped up and threw herself into my arms, kissing me on the cheek.

"I'm going to do my homework!" she exclaimed as she was already halfway down the hall.

"Elena!" I yelled after her.

"Yeeeeeahhhh?"

"Don't leave your bag on the armchair. You know Mum doesn't like that! And put your shoes away!"

12. SEATS OF POWER

Do you remember when I told you at the beginning that this book is dishonest? Now it's time to look at why, and I'll use my favourite scapegoat.

Aristotle had many faults. Let's start by listing a few, since they are pretty serious, considering he's the most influential person in history.

Yes, it's the fault of the person who was called *the brain* by Plato, his teacher, that biology as a science exists. It was created while Aristotle was bored in exile on an island.

And it was him who, after many centuries, influenced the European Enlightenment when his writings translated into Arabic were discovered in Toledo. He was a true genius, exceptional philosopher and scientist, who wrote volumes of logic, physics and philosophy, but also collections of moral and political works, the first real organic study on the subject. He also dabbled in poetry, just because he didn't know what else to do.

He produced an enormous body of work, investigating logic through the systematic observation of an event to explain the inexplicable at that time to his contemporaries.

Aristotle is responsible for the greatest of faults: that of having created the dialectic, as we call it today. Yes, he's guilty of having devised the sophisticated mechanisms that allow us human beings to converse and compromise in complex situations, guilty of having taught us to think.

This burdens all of us with the responsibility to always seek dialogue to resolve conflicts, of whatever kind, at any level. Aristotle is guilty of having theorised that we must assume our responsibilities and not dump them on others: *I don't know* and *I don't understand* are not acceptable excuses.

People who read know a lot; people who observe know much more, he said.

He also argued that we must explain things – even the most complicated things – in the simplest way possible, speaking like everybody speaks: think like wise men, but speak like ordinary people. He strongly believed in logic – understood as the power of word, the ability to argue intelligently and knowledgably, but without exaggerating. In fact, he argued that: *First you have to live, and then you can philosophise.* Force – understood as violence – and ignorance – understood as a lack of knowledge but also apathy – are the worst answers that can be given.

The ones that only those unable know how to offer. And even worse than those is indifference. Silence has always favoured the executioner, the oppressor, never the victim.

Violence is not only physical, but also verbal, which is often more subtle and devious. It makes us forget who we are: human beings capable of dialogue. Instead of raising their voices in a TV debate, many screamers should improve their arguments because by shouting, they alienate young people. It's one thing to go to a nightclub or to a party where the music is blaring, but the true intensity is deep, internal; it's another thing to be deafened by those who scream by saying nothing, just noise.

Young people are tired of being told that the world sucks. They are well aware of the difference between saying that it's bad and feeling discontented: music makes them feel good, even when it makes them feel bad. Getting in tune with the young mind is not a question of volume but of intensity of thought, of wavelength. The young people of today are not so different from us young people of yesterday or from those before us. Judging their pain or suffering based on the volume of those who shout makes us dull to all those who suffer in silence.

Furthermore, it's mainly men who raise their voices in political debates, perhaps because they're used to driving, shouting that they have right of way and expecting to have it even when they don't.

They scream that they're not screaming even when they're told that *they are* screaming, deaf from the ignorance of their statements. All young people want to change the world and the most positive changes in history have always occurred when this will was expressed. The most serious tragedy would be for apathy to take over.

One of my favourite writers, Ennio Flaiano, once wrote that *almost all young people have the courage of the opinions of others.* This clearly paints the boldness of young minds, always ready to speak before knowing a subject well, to run before being able to walk. At the same time, however, how many old people have I met who repeated the same mistakes for years, unable to evolve, to mature.

There's an African proverb that says *the youth can walk faster but the elder knows the road.*

Responsibility falls on those who are older, always.

Using age as an argument to silence somebody is something that has always bothered me, especially when I found myself having to deal with people unable to grow up, and I mean mentally, not physically.

We're only young once, but some people remain immature much longer. We always criticise young people, forgetting that when we were young, we were subjected to the same treatment, and we too needed examples more than criticism.

I was born in a generation that when asked *what do you want to do when you grow up?* always thought *I didn't know you could choose!* My parents dreamed of me becoming a judge or a lawyer. I disappointed them well and systematically, since I didn't want to disappoint them by not disappointing them.

As a child who was always accused of inconstancy and recklessness, I learnt that the fundamental rule of remaining a good parent is to be as consistent as possible, even if wrong. Better not to correct a small mistake so as to remain consistent, rather than contradict to fix something insignificant.

If any of you think by now that I am too protective of young people, you'd be very wrong. I have no qualms about scolding them when needed.

Every morning I'm up at five and a little before seven I'm at the bar enjoying my double shot of coffee.

One of those mornings, I arrived a little earlier than usual and while I was waiting for the shutters to open, an old man passed by and joyfully wished me good morning.

"Early riser!" I replied just as cheerfully.

The old man stopped and turned back.

"Are you off to work?" he asked me.

"Yes," I replied.

"Couldn't you give my nephew a job? You know, he was fired."

"I'm sorry. I work abroad…" I murmured.

"God bless you!" he replied discouraged.

As he walked away, I asked him what his grandson does, obviously referring to what work he did.

"He's sleeping," he replied, adding, "God help him!"

"And may Jesus throw him out of bed to look for work!" I found myself exclaiming.

A world where the old work and the young sleep has never been seen before. But let's remember that this is a world where those who worked hard for the end of Communism then found themselves unprepared when it collapsed.

A friend reading this book called it a humorous *Bignami* of doing politics in Italy, referring to that precious textbook that helped so many students to understand not only the *Risorgimento*, but also the history of the Roman Empire and Petrarch. I wish I could have made a *Bignami* of politics, but any attempt to make so much information pocket-sized in a minimum number of pages is truly impossible.

Therefore, the premise of this book – what is explained in large letters on the cover – must be understood in the first sense of the word in the Treccani vocabulary book: *to unfold, to spread out what was folded or enveloped, so that the entire surface is open and stretched, and visible.* And if we look for the figurative meaning of the word *explain*, we find this a little further: *open, spread: spread the wings, referring to birds, unfold them to fly, and, by extension, take flight, fly with spread wings, even in a figurative sense: But my lord, like a divine eagle, Behind the new wise men, take flight* (Parini).

The aim of this literary effort is to inspire young people – as Cristina and I do with our children – to think about everything, including politics, with their own head and not listen to what is normally said that has become commonplace.

We must always insist on not being afraid to undertake conversations that lead to an exchange of ideas, ensuring that individual freedom and the inalienable rights of all are protected.

The more banal meaning of *explain*, that is, *to make understand, to clarify, to make something obscure and difficult to understand clear and intelligible*, comes much later.

It's not a priority, neither in the vocabulary book nor here.

The most perverse form of control is to keep people ignorant, or to make them believe that some things are too complicated and should be left to insiders. But remember that knowing a bit about mechanics helps you to be a better driver and you don't need much knowledge.

If you hear a noise coming from your car, you shouldn't just turn up the volume of the radio and hope it'll go away. It's better to find out whether there are leaves trapped in the air duct or if it's the sound of a punctured tire. I assure you that while the leaves are only annoying, the punctured tire can cause some serious damage.

And speaking of damage, it's necessary to recognise what is presented in politics as damage when it's actually only damaging for those who can't take advantage of it.

And at the same time, not to turn every piece of news into a fact that really happened, especially in these times of media chaos. Spreading the word and maintaining the false myth that all politicians are corrupt and that politics is dirty does great harm, not only because it's unfair to those who serve their country competently, honestly and consciously, but also because doing this encourages people with few scruples to take advantage, thinking that everybody does the same thing.

Even worse, the person who has been honest up to now might cease to be honest because *I'm the only one*. I've met politicians who are extremely honest and morally upright, people who really wanted to make improvements that everybody could benefit from.

The most dangerous thing – and I say this as an emigrant – is to disparage an entire race, region or group just because a single element that belongs to it is a bad apple.

For every Totò Riina or Bernardo Provenzano – Sicilian mobsters – there is Giovanni Falcone, Peppino Impastato, Rocco Chinnici, Paolo Borsellino, Calogero Zucchetto, Ninni Cassarà, Rosario Livatino and many others, yet how many times do you hear people say that *all Sicilians are mafia*?

You realise that your children have grown up when they ask you questions that you can give answers to, and it's up to us to provide them or, in any case, enable them to know how or where to look for those answers.

As a parent, I need to be able to see *beyond*, not just *before* them. This does not have to translate into keeping them tied down; rather, we must set them free if we truly want them to stay close to us. The greatest gift we can give them is enthusiasm, without ever pouring out our frustrations and bitterness for the things that we haven't achieved.

Young people live off ideals and often see things in black and white, but as I've already written elsewhere, *black and white is good for the grey matter.*

In my years on film and advertising sets, I've seen many young people give their all and fail because they've given in to compromises sold by others as truths or shortcuts.

I left Italy in my twenties because I was told that I'd have to wait until my hair turned white to gain a position of responsibility and that notion terrified me even more when I looked around and saw that all the people in positions of responsibility really did have white hair.

White with fear, I collected my few belongings and went where they look at *what* you can do, not *who* has sent you or how old you are and what you've done up until now.

Filmmaking has taught me that the only real value I have as a bargaining chip is my name, that is, the integrity and competence that defines me.

Journalism and writing in general made me understand that we can't explain anything to anybody.

We can only live and tell others of our experiences, hoping that readers will benefit from them, or that at least we can make them reason with us.

Explaining makes no sense, and as Longanesi said, *a true journalist explains very well what he doesn't know.*

So, here's the dishonesty of this book: my awareness of not knowing enough, even when those around me tell me otherwise. Believing in people who only compliment us is dangerous in any profession, especially in politics: we feel a great warmth and a feeling of wellbeing, but remember that pee cools down quickly.

And now I'll explain, in the most common meaning of the term, why I know about politics.

As mentioned in the introduction, I have a sister who understands perfectly well how the Italian political machine works because she has worked in politics at the highest level for many years. If they weren't confidential and private, our chats would produce a beautiful and fascinating book, but Luisa doesn't like to be in the spotlight and I want to respect her discretion. Basically, that's what has made her so vital to so many of these powerful figures over the last thirty years.

Through her, I've met as many wonderful people, great connoisseurs not only of the Italian political soul, but also of the human soul. I don't mention their names here because I was asked not to.

Their suggestions when drafting these pages were invaluable and I admired their consummate experience and generosity, as well as their real and rare honesty not just in the political sphere.

Lastly, I must recognise an advantage that I've acquired over many years of life and admit that, thanks to age, I have more hours of experience than other people.

This advantage also comes from having done a job that has a lot of affinities with politics, not to mention identical mechanisms: filmmaking.

The link between the world of entertainment and politics is historical: *panem et circenses*, if you have forgotten it, is the cynical formula adopted since the time of the ancient Romans to control the masses.

The real secret of governing. If you think that film business is a game of deceptions, so is politics, but these deceptions are not necessarily made to harm, quite the contrary. The entertainment world has the same bargaining chip as the political world, the *name* – understood as reputation – the most valuable currency. Exchanging favours is the order of the day, not to mention that everybody is willing to do your job, not only for free but also for a fee.

Furthermore, only the most glamorous aspect is seen, always suspecting that somebody has achieved their position thanks to who knows what tricks and compromises.

Does that remind you of anything? So-called *show business* – a term that best captures everything that makes a show, not just filmmaking – is made up of continuous bargaining, where people hug you just to touch your back and feel the best place to stab you later calmly, away from prying eyes.

The similarity between the two *arts* has long been recognised, and you'll find it acknowledged by others who know much more than me, such as Paul Bengala, former adviser to Bill Clinton, who said *politics is show business for ugly people.*

In show business, loyalty lasts as long as your popularity, and self-celebration is a must, so much so that if the applause doesn't come, events are created to produce it.

For this reason, if you want to maintain a long career in show business, it's best not to believe all the compliments and awards you'll receive. It's better to keep your feet on the ground, always.

In politics, this is a must, so much so that in the days of ancient Rome, there was a slave who held the laurel of victory over the general's head, whispering in his ear as he passed through the adoring crowd: *Respice post te! Hominem te memento!* – Look behind you! Remember that you're only a man.

If you want to be in politics, don't drive a car; take the tube, the bus or, better still, walk. Observe the people around you closely. Remember that you're like everybody else. I've always thought that when somebody lifts you up on a pedestal, it's always so that others can take better aim.

172

Another unwanted advantage came after I emigrated to England. It wasn't a simple decision, and it was dictated by financial reasons, as is the case for most people who emigrate. When I hear that they don't want young people to move countries, I agree. Of course, it would be better for the country itself to change, but until that happens, it's inevitable.

Living abroad, however, gives you an advantage in observing your own people. It's like being on a boat, sitting with your feet in the water, still in contact with your origins, but at the same time able to look further, especially with respect to those who swim. The emigrant loves his country so deeply and suffers because he often has to defend it from those who laugh at it. But at the same time, he sees its defects because he has the detachment of those who are not on the water.

When I've been asked in the past to explain something about Italy or what it means to be Italian, I've almost always managed to get away with a joke, hoping that making somebody laugh for a few seconds would make them think longer.

And that's exactly what I've been trying to do here, to give some food for thought.

By sharing these cheerful chats with my children, I don't wish to change how they think, but get them to think that they are the ones who can change things, who can repair the damage we've done, our generations.

Finally, some words addressed to a particular type of reader. Don't be offended.

The subtitle of this book is *how to gain seats of power in Italy*, and I have the vague feeling that there will be people who buy this book hoping to find the secret of how to get into politics and obtain a position in some company or institution by wolfing down all the information here.

Although there are some tips buried within the pages of this book that I hope many will find useful when approaching the political world, I must disappoint shortcuts lovers.

Because the best way to rise to power is with honesty and fairness, always keeping in mind the reason why and who should be served once you gain a seat of power: the citizen.

By citizen, I mean people who work honestly, pay taxes and respect others, get up to go to work every day with dedication and the knowledge that taxes deducted from their salary or paid as an entrepreneur or freelancer help everybody, especially people who are less fortunate by birth or accident.

The responsibility of being in government – be it national or local, in any position, at any level – is enormous because every day you must demonstrate that you deserve the trust of those who voted for you.

My father worked excessively his whole life, including holidays, because many of his generation grew up with a sense of duty that was sometimes exaggerated.

One day, when I was grown up and had started work already, we discovered that he had not received a pay rise for several years, despite his responsibilities having increased.

We asked him why he had never asked for a pay rise.

After much insistence, he replied in a relatively agitated voice: "... because if I deserved it, they would have given it to me without me having to ask."

There you go.

The day you rise to power, remember my father and people like him, who got up every morning at five and came back late, tired, full of fatigue without ever complaining.

Remember, as you move the papers on your beautiful desk, that there are people much older or much younger than you who move huge loads every day without complaining.

When somebody brings you coffee at the office, always thank them.

Always thank them and be grateful to everybody. Somebody sewed the dress you're wearing, clicked the heels of your shoes, cooked the lunch you enjoyed so much with your colleagues.

Above all, remember that the weight on that seat of power is the weight of responsibility and promises made to those who believe in you, who every day hope that you will be the one who turns their lives around.

Finally, don't forget that you too were young, and that not finding answers to the questions you were looking for was frustrating and alienating. Be willing to share your experience, knowledge and privilege of power with others as you sit high on your throne. And never forget, at any time, that the throne is not that high and your feet touch the floor, so you'd better keep them on the ground.

EPILOGUE

When I was revising my notes to write this book, I came across a little card from my daughter, written when she was just five years old: *I love you daddy!* Words written in coloured pencil, accompanied by flowers and hearts, which adorn the dreams of all little princesses.

I've always travelled a lot. My work is cruel on loved ones and even if my children have become used to my sudden disappearances over the years, it's never been easy.

On her first day of school, I told Elena that I wouldn't be able to take her because I had to catch a flight early that morning. Her mother would wait for her outside school.

She sighed with the conscious seriousness of her six years.

"Dad..." she said in a faint voice. "Why do you always have to go away?"

"To work, I have to earn money."

"What do you need money for?"

"So that I can buy you clothes, feed you and pay to send you to school."

She paused, gripped me in a tighter hug and then, all in one breath, she said.

"Dad, I can always wear this dress, I'll eat less and I don't like school."

My eyes tear up just thinking about it.

I also remember the expression on the passport control officer's face at London airport as he was covered in a shower of glitter and dust that came out when he opened my passport. It contained an apology note from Elena for not saying goodbye to me because I would be leaving too early the next day. Seeing my horrified expression, the gruff officer flashed a rare smile and, with true British aplomb, he returned everything by saying that he too had a young daughter.

I have cards and notes everywhere. I keep one inside the transparent case of my mobile phone as a cover. It only has a little heart and the word *love*, which more than once has made me the object of mischievous smiles in many quarters.

A note from Elena has become a precious bookmark on my Kindle. And if you're wondering how it's possible to have a physical bookmark on an e-book, we must be worlds apart in our style of reading.

I realise that the time has come for me to write her a note too. That in years to come, it will continue to spread brilliance wherever it goes, that it will survive technology and that it will always make you smile and think, even when there's little to laugh about and so much to say again.

Dear Elena,

I'll hold my words for a moment longer so that I can warm them up a bit before leaving them to you.

I have no trail to follow. Nobody prepares a father to provide certainties and you must always be wary of people who offer answers that are convenient and made for the moment. They're often stolen from the writings of others, misinterpreted and translated for their own benefit.

I'm writing to you here because I have a past. I'm writing to you now because you're the future.

Look at history and remember that it actually doesn't repeat itself. The past tells us things only once. We might think it's already happened, but that's because we don't listen to it. Don't look back too often; it'll give you a stiff neck.

Pay no heed to people who shout. You'll only encourage their lack of ideas or, worse, their dangerous ignorance.

Pay attention to people who give you advice but do your own thing by following your heart.

That way, if you make a mistake, you will not blame your head, to which we forgive little or nothing.

You can only improvise if you're well prepared and if you're not, then it'll always be your fault. Don't blame others for your own negligence. Don't dress it up with creativity by hiding behind the face of an artist. Those who are creative don't need to say so.

Choose your battles. Find your own *dragon* to fight. Don't support causes you don't believe in, just to please the overbearing or the majority.

If everybody zigs, nobody stops you from zagging, and it might be even more fun as long as you don't do both too often. Going straight is relative to the length of the road. The greater the distance, the less sharp the bend.

Remember that order doesn't mean authority and that we must also obey what the laws don't explicitly say, as long as it makes sense, because it imposes shame on us, as Seneca once said.

Good sense is not necessarily common sense.

Question, if necessary, what most people passively accept out of laziness alone. It's okay to relax, but it's best to do it like every mother does with her puppies.

Defend the weak, but don't let people take advantage of your generosity. Helping does not mean blindly assisting; it means enabling the person to get up on their own, with dignity, but above all putting them back on their feet so that they can help others, not just themselves.

Respect different cultures and religions, but don't allow anybody to impose theirs on you. You also have full right not to believe and not to agree.

Shun fanaticism, whatever colour it may have, especially if it's a celebration of nostalgia. Memories are beautiful if they remain memories. Fanatics want a law that, applied literally to everything and everybody, distributes heaven or hell. They obtusely ignore the fact that a law must be interpreted, no writing is objective and that human beings are an exception by definition.

Respect people who work and reject slackers. Laziness is the most dangerous vice that exists because people who don't want to do always look for shortcuts, to the detriment of others.

Don't jump to conclusions when you hear news. Make sure the facts are really as reported. Check multiple sources. Don't make conclusions based on hearsay. Believe in who was present, but not entirely.

Don't judge by appearances. I only ever used one pair of shoes until they broke, although I could have bought two.

Don't throw away what can be fixed.

Remember that intervening in areas where you lack expertise is not only dangerous, but you risk looking incompetent. It's up to the police to arrest criminals, lawyers to defend them and it's only judges who convict or acquit.

Respect institutions, but remember that they're at the service of everybody, including you, and they're not above anyone despite their high-sounding titles.

Follow the economy and understand its mechanisms. Don't waste money, but know when it's time to spend rather than die and become the richest person in the cemetery.

Making sacrifices for the common good is always worthwhile.

Cultivate friendships, but don't put your friends before the values you respect. A true friend walks beside you, not in front of you.

Respect your colleagues and those you work with. You're only as fast as the slowest in your group and you're only good because others recognise it or allow it.

Remember that you can't control what others do to you, but you can control your reaction, and that doesn't always mean smiling.

Love your family. Surround them with books – they are the best form of protection and wealth. Ignorant people know only poverty. A book lights up the mind, and it's a light that nobody can switch off.

Be interested in new technologies and make them your own. You have to understand enough about them so that if you're told that it can't be done, you can object.

Don't be impressed by the performance of a car.

Always ask for the best driver and make sure he has children that he wants to hug at the end of the race.

Don't take a person's hope away – it may be all they have left – but don't make promises you can't keep.

Apologise if necessary, but don't overdo it in public. Shake the hand that is offered to you, even if you don't respect an idea, so you can always make your strength and resolve felt.

Listen to music, cook your own food and play sports. Love animals as if they were people, but respect their nature because they are not human beings.

Defend the environment. The world is not only small, but also the only one we have and we can't go anywhere else. We can't change the air.

Love Italy and be proud of being Italian. Think of all the foreigners who wish they had been born here.

How many Italians do you know who wish they hadn't?

Remember that your mum and dad have tried to err as little as possible, but they haven't always succeeded, although your mother has actually made less mistakes.

Love

Babbo

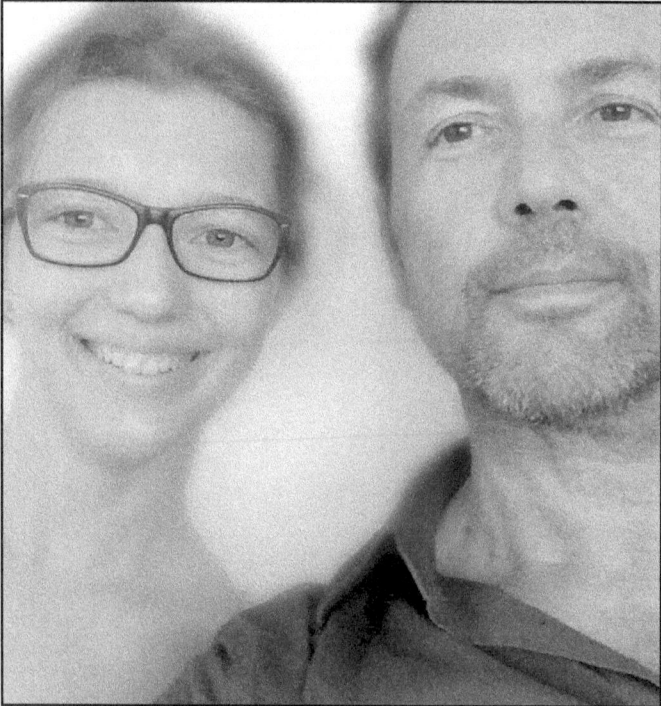

Francesco (Franz) Pagot with Elena.

FRANCESCO (FRANZ) PAGOT was born in Conegliano and studied at *Liceo Classico* at a time when pupils still had to translate from Greek to Latin. After working for several years in advertising and cinema, he moved to London, assisting on masterpieces such as Full Metal Jacket, before becoming a well-known and respected cinematographer, making numerous films and more than five hundred commercials. He has worked with such film legends as Peter O'Toole, Ray Winstone, Jude Law and Giancarlo Giannini. He is an esteemed painter and some of his works are on display at the Saatchi Art Collection.

He is a member of the prestigious BAFTA, the English equivalent of Oscar, and is a registered journalist in England, with war zone experience. He has won numerous awards and published several books. He occasionally teaches in various schools and universities and he is in great demand as a communication speaker across the world. Married with two children, he lives between London and Italy. In 2018, he was awarded a Knighthood.

www.ingramcontent.com/pod-product-compliance
Lightning Source LLC
Chambersburg PA
CBHW032106280326
41933CB00009B/769